MW01289549

the PROCESS of *Holiness*

CARLA BURTON

2015 Copyright © Carla Burton.

All Scripture quotations in this book are from the King James Version of the Bible unless otherwise noted.

All rights reserved. No portion of this publication may be reproduced, stored in an electronic system, or transmitted in any form or by any means, electronic, mechanical, photocopy, recording, or otherwise, without prior permission of Carla Burton.

ISBN-13: 978-1517636319

DEDICATION

This book is dedicated to my parents, Carl and Joann Varnell.

Everything I know about holiness I learned from watching their godly example. They never made it an issue of dress but rather an issue of the heart! I learned to love living for God in all my ways by watching them live it each day with joy!

Thank you, Dad, for putting this truth in my heart! Thank you, Mom, for living it with joy until the day you went to be with the Lord. I dedicate every word written and learned to your example!

Table of Contents

Preface

Being raised in the church, I have always obediently and to the best of my ability followed holiness standards. However, when my husband and I took our present church in Nashville, Tennessee, I quickly realized that I was going to be teaching others how they should live. Feeling the great responsibility of teaching God's Word correctly, I began a personal study into the subject of holiness. During this time, the Lord gave me great revelation concerning the process of holiness. I began to understand that what I believed was **all correct**, however, I had obeyed it in all the wrong order.

I have written this book so that anyone, a new convert or a long-time Christian, can study and understand the order and importance of every aspect of holiness. My greatest desire is that through this book, you will be able to walk in holiness with great joy and understanding.

I do ask that as you read this book and "study to show yourself approved unto God" that you will do so with an open and willing heart. Your obedience to the Word is dependent upon your heart, spirit and mind being open to not only *hearing* but *doing* the Word of God.

ONE

An Open Heart

They say that there are three things that you never discuss unless you want to debate and they are: money, politics and religion. These are three areas that people have very definite opinions and are usually extremely verbal in expressing them. But if we take that same principle and define it within the Christian community, there is one topic that most Christian's have very "strong opinions" regarding – holiness. I have heard people, who never spoke up regarding any other Biblical subject have a vocal and defined opinion regarding this topic.

I believe that having a strong opinion is a great thing on any subject, as long as you have the right Biblical basis and understanding to back up your opinion. We have gotten ourselves in trouble throughout the history of man, by walking according to our own understanding rather than according to the Word of God.

There is a difference between being a hearer and a doer of the Word. But what is the difference? I believe that being a doer comes down to not just hearing and believing in the Word but also receiving an illumination of the principle and purpose of the commandment and then obedience follows.

For God to get His Word from creation to the Bible that we hold in our hands today, He had to create a process. There were three steps He used to accomplish this task.

> ➤ Revelation – from God to man *(man hears what God wants written)*
> ➤ Inspiration – from man to paper *(man becomes the scribe for God and writes what He wants told)*

> Illumination – from paper to heart *(man receives and obeys that which is written)*

It is not enough that we just have a revelation that God wants to tell us something or even an inspiration to read what has already been written, but we must have a personal, intense illumination from the Word for us to become obedient.

The apostle Paul was a perfect example of this in Acts chapter nine. Paul was raised a strict Pharisee and when he was approximately fourteen sent to Jerusalem to become a rabbi. He sat and learned at the feet of Gamaliel, one of the most prominent teachers of that day. He grew up strong in his belief that the Holy Scriptures were given by revelation of God and he never questioned the men who had written these Scriptures through inspiration. But Paul still did not have an illumination of Jesus Christ. However, following his experience on the road to Damascus, Paul becomes a man of understanding and obedience.

This new illuminated Paul was so adamant about this that he wrote the following in ~~Galatians 1:8-9,~~ *"But though we, or an angel from heaven, preach any other gospel unto you than that which we have preached unto you, let him be accursed. As we said before, so say I now again, If any man preach any other gospel unto you than that you have received, let him be accursed."* These are truly the words of a man who has received a divine illumination regarding the Scriptures.

The purpose of this book is not to give you a personal opinion regarding holiness but rather to give you a guide *from the Bible* to help you find illumination. All I ask is that as you walk through this process of holiness that you sincerely, earnestly and with an open heart and mind, seek understanding regarding this topic. Allow the written Word to become illuminated in your heart through the process of study and then your actions will follow.

TWO

Submission to Authority

The Bible has one theme throughout its entirety and that is submitting our will to the will of God and the authority that He places in our lives. I will never be able in this chapter to give you a complete, Biblical understanding of authority and the importance of your submission to that authority, but you do need to understand the purpose of submission in regards to holiness.

First of all I would like to make myself clear regarding this book and the authority of your Pastor. My desire, in this book, is to give you knowledge and understanding but not to give you a tool to use against your Shepherd. God has placed the man of God in our lives to lead, guide and instruct us in the ways of righteousness more perfectly. There may be standards discussed here, that your Pastor has required something more or different from you and your church. It is very important that you remember that God placed you in that flock and under that Shepherd to guide your life and the *greatest holiness standard you can follow is submission to the authority* in your life! Now, let me be very clear here, if your pastoral authority is asking you to do things that cannot be backed up by Scripture, or the importance to the overall good of your local assembly cannot be explained, then you need to seek the counsel of godly men and through prayer and fasting make a decision regarding this. However, if your Pastor is teaching you from the Word of God and the problem is that you don't agree but cannot back it up Biblical, then you need to check *your* spirit. That is a spirit of rebellion and you need to be sure that you are submitted to the godly authority in your life.

I remember when I was growing up, one Sunday my Pastor, T. L. Craft from Jackson, Mississippi got up and his sermon that day was,

"Thou Shalt Not Play Rook!" Of course, the entire church sat up and took notice because this was a favorite game of the young married couples and the singles. But our Pastor went on to explain by telling us that this was not a heaven or hell standard but that this was a request by him that we would abstain from this on a temporary basis. He further elaborated by saying that the reason he did this was because our young married and singles were staying up on Saturday nights until the wee hours of the morning playing marathon Rook games and then sleeping in and missing church and their ministry duties on Sunday morning. He used scriptures about faithfulness, the Bible's command to not miss the opportunity to assemble in a church environment, the Old Testament scriptures about placing other "idols" before your relationship with God.

Now you may think that is ridiculous or he should not have done that. I disagree with you. God had placed that man in charge of the spiritual wellbeing of those saints. He was going to have to give an account for their souls and his desire was to be able to do it with joy and not sorrow (Hebrews 13:17). The true test of this message was that God began, at that moment, testing the submission of the people to the godly authority placed in their lives. Submission to godly, Biblical-based authority is as important, sometimes more important, than the standard. What I mean is that sometimes God sets the "issue and/or standard" aside to deal with the concept of submission to authority in your life.

I want to be sure that you understand how important the issue of spiritual authority is to me because I never want this book to be used as a tool against your Pastor. No matter my personal opinion, God has placed that man of God in your life and you should respect, love and follow his instructions. This book is simply a tool to help you find the Biblical basis for why we believe what we believe and to help you understand the principle behind the issue. This is not a tool to help you subvert spiritual authority in your life.

THREE

Order by God

God plans *everything*. In I Corinthians 14:40 the Apostle Paul insists, *"Let all things be done decently and in order."* Even before the world was created, God knew exactly how He would order the planets, how He would have to redeem the world back unto Himself, and how He would have to dwell in man to help him maintain order in his walk with God upon this earth.

There is power in God's order. Read Ecclesiastes 3:1-8. The scripture explains how God has ordered the seasons of life. He has given everything a time, place, and way. We must never underestimate the power of God's order. We must not rush the times of weeping, mourning, breaking down, and war because without those things in their order we could not have laughing, dancing, building up, and love.

Here are some examples of things God has set in order: the seasons (Ecclesiastes 3:1); the Solar System (Genesis 1:15-17; Psalms 8:3; I Corinthians 15:40-41); the ecological and weather system (Job 36:27-28); and the chain of authority of God-Man-Woman (Genesis 1-3 and I Corinthians 11:2-3).

If God took the time to show us through all of His works that things should be done in a specific order, then why would holiness not have a proper order as well? By walking through each of these steps in order, you will find the process of illumination beginning to take place in your life. The ordered steps of holiness are: getting the right **attitude**, understanding the Biblical **principle** behind the issue and then putting these two into actions by obeying the **standard**.

FOUR

Defining The Steps

Attitude

An attitude is "a mental position or feeling with regard to a fact or state; the position of something in relation to something else." (*Webster's Dictionary*, Landoll, 1997) An attitude involves an understanding that holiness is a part of God and a part of Himself that He wants to give to us. Only when we have that understanding can we fulfill the second half of the definition of attitude—relating it to something else. When our minds take on an attitude of holiness, then we can relate that attitude to our daily lives and actually produce a holy lifestyle.

Principles

A principle is "a fundamental law, doctrine, or assumption; a rule or code of conduct and a devotion to that conduct; a primary source; an active source." (*Webster's Dictionary*, Landoll, 1997) A principle involves our knowledge and reason for following a code of conduct. It is the underlying law or doctrine that we understand and then obey according to our understanding. Once we understand the doctrine or law, then we can apply the second part of the definition of principle to our lives. When we have the knowledge, then it becomes the primary source that activates our lifestyle.

Standards

A standard is "something set up as a rule for measuring or as a model to be followed." (*Webster's Dictionary*, Landoll, 1997) A standard involves a person's body acting upon the knowledge of the principle, which is fueled by his or her mind having the right attitude concerning the fact.

FIVE

Attitude

Before we begin discussing attitude, let's understand that attitude is a condition of the heart. But attitude also *ALWAYS* shows up on the outside! Ever had to discipline your child? How about had a disagreement with your spouse? Ever forgot an important date or event? Ever said about someone, "They are so negative"? Have you ever seen someone talking and even though you couldn't hear what was being said, you could tell what kind of attitude they had? Ever had your child stomp around or slam a door? Ever had your spouse continually and deeply sigh to let you know they weren't pleased about something? If you have answered yes to any of these – then you understand that attitudes always make themselves known outwardly.

Proverbs 23:7 says, *"As a man thinketh in his heart so is he."* That is strong language when you realize that your attitude controls your actions. Your attitude controls your emotions and your attitude controls your obedience. Let's look at some examples:

> ➤ Adam – a man who couldn't live in a perfect place with only one commandment.
> ➤ Moses – a murderer, and a man who didn't have the confidence to speak for himself.
> ➤ Abraham – a guy who didn't want to be patient for the promise of God to come to pass.
> ➤ Jacob/Israel – a deceiver and master manipulator.
> ➤ Rahab – a harlot
> ➤ Eli – a preacher who couldn't control his own home.
> ➤ King David – an adulterer and conspirator to murderer.
> ➤ King Solomon – a man who was influenced by the woman he allowed into his life.

➤ Samson – a young man who couldn't control his own desires.
➤ Peter – an impetuous, outspoken, quick to anger young man.
➤ James & John, sons of Zebedee – very position oriented men.
➤ Paul – a strong willed and extremely opinionated man.

Don't confuse being flawed with having a bad attitude. Just because we have weaknesses and personal issues does not mean that we cannot have the right attitude. God's choice of people throughout the Bible shows us that He doesn't worry about flaws, but He does check out our attitude.

A perfect example is how Jesus dealt with the Pharisee's. When they came to him, they always came with a spirit of rebellion, debate, to create confusion, to try and trip Him up and to prove themselves right. They came with a judgmental, self-righteous attitude. Jesus dealt with them by not even entertaining their conversations. He called them out on their motives and their purpose. He consistently pointed out the problems with their words and actions and how the two didn't always match up. Jesus never reached to use them or called them to follow Him.

But what was different about Nicodemus, a Pharisee that we see in John chapter three? The difference was in his attitude. We know this because his attitude showed up in his actions in approaching Jesus. He approached Him humble, with an open and willing mind and heart, and a desire to really know the truth (John 3:2). Because of that Jesus dealt with him differently than the other Pharisee's. He begins to explain the plan of salvation in depth. From this conversation we get some of the most powerful scriptures for salvation that continue to illuminate our lives today. The right attitude makes all the difference in the world.

The Wrong Attitude

We talked about Biblical examples of men that were flawed but able to be used by God because of the right inward attitude. But now we have to see the difference of men in the Bible that were rejected by God because of the wrong attitude. You must understand these men had the same opportunities as those around them but their attitude determined their action and both were not pleasing to God.

> ➤ Cain – a man who thought he knew better than God

> ➤ Esau – a man who didn't treasure the things of God.
> ➤ Achan – a greedy man
> ➤ King Saul – an impatient, prideful man
> ➤ King Rehoboam – a foolish man who followed bad counsel (yet the son of the wisest man alive, Solomon)
> ➤ Judas – an arrogant deceitful man who tried to force the plan of God.
> ➤ Rich, young ruler – a church going, scripture believing man who had put other things first before God.

When you look at the lives of these men, the difference between this list and the previous one comes down to one thing – their attitude. One list of men was flawed but had a teachable attitude. The other list was also flawed but was unwilling to learn.

The life of Cain and Able is the clearest example of this difference. They were brothers and were raised in the same home environment. They heard their parents tell the story of the garden and their sin of disobedience. They heard about how that because of this sin they had to leave the garden and work to be able to provide for their family. They heard about how that before God allowed them to leave the garden, He gave an object lesson on what they had to do to create an atmosphere where His presence could come and communicate with them. Genesis 3:21 is one of the most overlooked scriptures in the Bible. This is where God showed them by killing an animal, shedding it's blood and making a coat of skin to cover the outward symbol of the inward sinful change, that they were able to create a temporary bridge back into fellowship with Him. They obviously understood this lesson and passed it down to their sons, Cain and Able. Because we see, in Genesis 4:3-4, that they each set up an altar and brought an offering unto God. The difference was Able followed the instruction manual and offered the right sacrifice, but Cain followed the sin of his father and mother and thought he could do it his way. God even gave him a chance to change it all before he continued down this path (Genesis 4:6-7). And how amazing that his attitude was seen outwardly because God asks him why his countenance (facial expression) had fallen. But because Cain did not have a teachable attitude, God could not use him and his life becomes cursed (Genesis 4:11-12). I want you to understand that these two young men had almost everything in common – same home, same teaching, same environment, same knowledge, and the same work ethic. But those things are not what determined their usefulness to God – it was in one's submitted, teachable attitude versus the others rebellious, unwilling-to-learn attitude. There is a saying, *"A bad attitude is like a flat tire, until you fix it you are going nowhere."* So remember attitude determine obedience and your usefulness to God.

Holiness without a holy attitude makes a person's holiness *standards* nothing in His eyes.

God's Judgment of our Attitude

God will judge our attitude, whether good or bad, useful or unusable. Jesus showed us throughout the Bible that He rewards good, teachable attitudes. In the examples of the men found with a good attitude we see that God used them in spite of their flaws but because He knew they could be taught and learn. Adam the first sinner but also the first redeemed by the shedding of blood. Moses the murderer was also the deliverer of the nation of Israel. Jacob the deceiver was also the father of Judah, the lineage of Christ. King David a man who committed a very grievous sin but God chose to anoint the son of that relationship as the next King (Bathsheba was Solomon's mother) and he was the only man called "a man after God's own heart". Samson a man who lost it all because he couldn't control his own desires was given another chance. His hair grew back, his strength returned and he was used by God to destroy more

Philistines. Peter the one who emphatically denied Christ was the one chosen only 50 days later to preach the first message of salvation on the day of Pentecost (Acts 2). Paul the man who held the coat at Stephen's stoning became one of the greatest missionaries of the gospel and the writer of most of the New Testament. A good, teachable attitude will allow God to use your life.

The parable of the talents found in Matthew 25:14-30 shows us the contrast of God's judgment regarding attitude. They each received something from the master. But when he returned, only two had been useful to Him. He shows that He rewards the good and faithful servants but he condemns the slothful servant and calls him unprofitable or unusable. Just remember that your attitude will determine your judgment, so work to learn and obey.

But not only does he judge the usefulness of those with a good attitude, He also recognizes and rewards those with the wrong attitude. We see in our example of the wrong attitude, that the punishment was usually a complete separation from God's plan and presence in their lives. Cain was driven out from his family and his home. Esau lived in bitterness and anger for many years and was never given the opportunity to get the birthright back. Achan destroyed not only his own life but caused the death of his entire family. King Saul had the kingdom taken away from his lineage and wound up at the end consulting with witches to try and find the plan of God for his life. King Rehoboam took the advice of the wrong counselors and wound up losing all but a small portion of the Kingdom of Israel. Judas wound up committing suicide because he was unable to come to terms with the choices he had made. The rich, young ruler was never heard from again in scriptures. How sad to see the lives of these men fall so far. But they had the same opportunity to learn and grow from their flaws and mistakes. The problem is that they could not be taught and because of this attitude they were unable to be used by God.

The issue with us today is all in our attitude about holiness. No matter your denomination or belief system, if we never stop learning from His Word, being kind to one another and working to be obedient in our own lives, then He will consider our attitude acceptable. For some the greatest issue is whether to receive the Word and be obedient to holiness. For others it is to judge those that do not adhere to all the teaching that they feel are important. The key is that we approach all scripture with an open heart and a willing mind and an obedient spirit. If we are working to develop ourselves with this concept then we can in turn help others when they have questions.

The Apostle Paul writes the following rebuke to the Christian church in Rome: *"But why dost thou judge thy brother? or why dost thou set at nought thy brother? for we shall all stand before the judgment seat of Christ. For it is written, As I live, saith the Lord, every knee shall bow to me, and every tongue shall confess to God. So then every one of us shall give account of himself to God. Let us not therefore judge one another any more: but judge this rather, that no man put a stumblingblock or an occasion to fall in his brother's way."* (Romans 14:10-13) Two things we need to understand is (1) You will give an account for yourself and your actions one day and (2) you need to work as hard at not judging or creating obstacles for your brother as you do about working on your own issues.

We are our brother's keepers and we will give account for our treatment of them one day. God showed us this when he demanded of Cain to account for his brother, Able. Cain tried to pass it off that he was not responsible to keep up with what happened to Able but God showed him differently in Genesis 4:10-12. God required Cain to pay for the death of his brother Able. No matter what you think, if you are responsible because of your attitude and/or actions in causing someone to quit following Christ, you will have to give an account for them one day. Just remember that you are responsible for yourself and for your actions towards others.

We will all be judged by Christ. In John 12:48 Jesus said, *"He that rejecteth me, and receiveth not my words, hath one that judgeth him: the word that I have spoken, the same shall **judge** him in the last day."* This is the most important thing to remember about our attitude. The first person that I have to give account for unto God is myself. I have to explain my attitude and defend my actions when I stand before God. Revelations 20:11-15 tells us that we will all stand before God and have to show that we did obey the Word of God, not only in our word but in our actions as well. So the greatest concern in my life is not what others are doing but rather what am I doing?

The Word of God must be our personal standard of judgment. We don't have time to go around and judge others when there is so much to learn from God's Word (II Corinthians 10:12). Instead we should strive to constantly align ourselves through obedience to the Word of God.

Everyone will give an account of his or her own life. God will require an explanation for every word or deed that was in error. I would hate to have to stand before God and explain why I had a bad attitude toward a brother or sister instead of a growing relationship with Him. He will probably respond to many people's feeble explanations with, *"What business was their life to yours?"*

In fact Jesus asked Peter this same question in John 21. He and Peter had this conversation about love and feeding His sheep and then in verse 18 Jesus begins to share the end of Peter's life with him. He was telling Peter how his death was going to glorify God. And Peter, not really liking how this conversation was going, turns to Jesus and asks Him about John the Beloved. Basically Peter said to Jesus, "What about John? How will he die?" And Jesus gives us once again this concept of being accountable for ourselves and not worrying about others by telling Peter, "What is to you if I let him live until I come back again?" We must understand that our responsibility is to live our lives compared to the Word of God and under submission to the godly authority in our lives. We have to be careful that we don't allow this judgmental society that we live in to creep into our walk as Christians. We must make sure that we are taking care of our lives and let God and the Pastor worry about everyone else.

We must avoid becoming a stumblingblock in another person's life. If we look like the holiest Pentecostal and yet our attitude stinks, offending our brothers and sisters in the Lord, then we are in direct disobedience to Romans 14:13. God will hold us accountable for our attitude. The blood of any soul lost as a result of our attitude will be upon our hands! **I don't want to stand before God with blood on my hands and try to explain it away.** You won't have to if you repent and get written in the book of life.

I have often said this regarding holiness. I don't care where you are on the journey (you may be at mile marker 100 while others are at mile marker 1,000) but what I am interested in is WHAT DIRECTION ARE YOU WALKING? If you are moving towards Christ then you are moving in the right direction. The closer you get into His presence you WILL put off things of the world – often without having to be asked to do it. Because of this I have to understand my responsibility as a Christian towards new converts or those just learning about Christ. You must get the picture of this in your mind. If they are on the road and they are moving in the direction of Christ, and I get in their face and begin to direct them on all the things they are doing wrong, where have I placed myself? I have become a stumblingblock or a roadblock or an obstacle in their continuing journey towards Christ. So many people are standing in the wrong place. They have actually placed themselves between the person and Christ. They have asked the new convert to take their eyes of Christ and look at them while they "straighten them out." We have to understand that when we do this we cause that person to stop walking towards God, focus on us and actually go over or around us to continue moving towards Christ.

Our responsibility is just the opposite. We are supposed to be standing behind that new convert encouraging them to continue moving in the direction they are. We need to be their best supporter and their greatest cheerleader! We need to be in their ears (not in front of their eyes) and we need to let them know they are walking in the right direction. Though they may not understand everything right now, just continue seeking God, reading His Word, praying for illumination and obeying what they understand.

Amen *Amen*

When we are in our proper place let me show you what will happen. If that person ever decides to turn around and move in the opposite direction; NOW I become a stumblingblock to them backsliding or turning from God. We must make sure that if we are going to be a stumblingblock to someone that we are what they have to get over to backslide and not to continue in their journey towards God.

Consequences of a Wrong Attitude

In Matthew 7:1-5, Jesus says, *"**Judge** not, that ye be not judged. For with what judgment ye judge, ye shall be judged: and with what measure ye mete, it shall be measured to you again. And why beholdest thou the mote that is in thy brother's eye, but considerest not the beam that is in thine own eye? Or how wilt thou say to thy brother, Let me pull out the mote out of thine eye; and, behold, a beam is in thine own eye? Thou hypocrite, first cast out the beam out of thine own eye; and then shalt thou see clearly to cast out the mote out of thy brother's eye."* (Emphasis added)

Galatians 6:7 describes the principle of sowing and reaping. Principles are things that WILL HAPPEN, not might or maybe, but WILL HAPPEN. There are principles in nature such as gravity (jump out an upper window in a tall building and see if the principle doesn't stand true) and the principle of the necessity of oxygen for life (try to breathe water and live). But even more than the principles of nature, spiritual principles established in the Word of God are more certain to be true. SPIRITUAL PRINCIPLES WILL ALWAYS COME TRUE!!! Sowing what we've reaped is an infallible principle of the Word. Adam and Eve sowed rebellion and disobedience when they ate the forbidden fruit and reaped it in sin and death; Jacob sowed deceit in his dealings with Esau and his father and reaped deceit when Laban switched Leah for Rachel; and Jesus told Peter in Matthew 26:51, *"...for all they that take the sword shall perish with the sword."* See also John 18:11

When we disobey the first half of Matthew 7:1, then we will reap the second half of Matthew 7:1. When we judge others, we can

----

expect to be judged, not only by people on this earth but also by God in heaven. See Matthew 7:2. If we constantly judge others, then we can't get upset when we become the topic of discussion somewhere else. **Don't load the gun and then get mad because you get shot with it.**

In Matthew 7:3-5, Jesus uses an absurd scenario. Why would we allow someone who is blind try to get something out of our eye? Anyone with a beam or log in his eye is blinded by that beam, just as someone who only sees holiness his or her own way is blind to further revelation or understanding—**not compromise, but *further understanding*.** If there are still things we are learning from the Bible about everything else, then there are still things that we can learn from the Bible concerning holiness. We cannot constantly try to get our brother or sister to line up with a holiness standard when we are suffering from the bigger problem of a holiness attitude problem.

In Matthew 23:13-28, Jesus delivers a rebuke to the Pharisees. He accuses them of shutting up the kingdom of heaven for others (v. 13) and seeking far and wide to make one convert then turning them into bitter, judgmental Pharisees just like themselves (v. 15). He calls them blind (vs. 16, 17, 19, 24, and 26) and tells them that their tithes and standards don't mean anything because they have forgotten mercy and judgment (v. 23). Then He sums it up with what relates best to the point of this lesson. He says in Matthew 23:24-28, *"Ye blind guides, which strain at a gnat, and swallow a camel.* ***Woe unto you, scribes and Pharisees, hypocrites!*** *for ye make clean the outside of the cup and of the platter, but within they are full of extortion and excess.* ***Thou blind Pharisee,*** *cleanse first that which is within the cup and platter, that the outside of them may be clean also.* ***Woe unto you, scribes and Pharisees, hypocrites! for ye are like unto whited sepulchres,*** *which indeed appear beautiful outward, but are within full of dead men's bones, and of all uncleanness. Even so ye also outwardly appear righteous unto men, but within ye are full of hypocrisy and iniquity."* Each of us should substitute our names in the place of the Pharisees to see if we have a problem with an attitude of holiness.

Attitude will determine how pleasing our holiness is to God. *The whole purpose of holiness is to be pleasing unto God and accepted into His presence so therefore a large part of our holiness is our attitude*. God was very specific in the Old Testament regarding the types and appearance of the sacrifices that were offered to Him. There were instances where someone brought a sacrifice but because they didn't offer the right one it was not accepted by Him.

In Genesis 4 we see Cain bring an offering. But God had no pleasure in Cain's offering, because he did not bring the correct one. Nadab and Abihu in Leviticus 10 offered strange fire to God and they were killed. We have to understand that many people have a strict holiness standard outwardly but inside their attitude sticks. God wants us to know that He looks at every part of us and needs to make sure that we are complete in ALL holiness standards. Your outward holiness will be acceptable to Him if your inward attitude is correct. Offer Him your attitude first and then get the rest in order.

Your Perspective Affects Your Attitude

The way a person feels about holiness will be related to how that person views holiness. Our attitude is always affected by our perspective (remember the "glass half empty versus glass half full concept?). The most important thing a person should remember is that God is our loving, Heavenly Father and only desires the best for His children. Matthew 7:9-11 reveals how much more God loves His children than even an earthly father would love his children. If a child asks his earthly father for bread, he wouldn't be given a stone; if a child asks his father for a piece of fish, he wouldn't be given a snake. Jesus says, *"If ye then, being evil, know how to give good gifts unto your children, how much more shall your Father which is in heaven give good things to them that ask him."* Even more than an earthly father, Jesus wants the best for His children and He wants them to be protected from harm.

Many people don't need to change their holiness standard they just need to change their own perspective regarding their obedience to holiness. Don't just continually clean your glasses if you cannot see, but go and get your prescription updated. So often the problem is not the standard but how we view our obedience to the standard. Change your perspective regarding holiness and all of the sudden you will realize a liberty you have never felt before.

Your Prison or Your Protection

Many people view holiness as a prison. A prison is a facility built to "keep people locked or bound inside." (*Webster's Dictionary*, Landoll, 1997) It is not a place that is viewed positively, but rather it is viewed as a place to avoid. The walls are built to keep people imprisoned or locked up so that they cannot escape and be free. If prison doors were opened, there would not be one prisoner who would remain, because it's not a place where people want to be.

When a person views holiness as a prison, then he or she will not view God as a loving father, but rather as a stern warden or taskmaster. If a person sees God as unjustly handing down sentences or standards, that person will spend all his time dreaming of escaping the prison. He will dread every moment he lives. His mind will invent ways in which he can be released.

But there are some barriers that are built for our protection. Barriers, such as fences, dams, and walls are built to protect us against predators, floods, animals, rain and other elements that might harm us. These things are put in our lives **not to keep us in, but to keep danger out**.

When my husband and I bought our first home our backyard was bordered by a wooded area. Our daughter, Caitlin, was about 4 years old and would not go out into the backyard to play or swing unless her father or I were with her. She kept telling us that she was afraid of what was in the woods. We invested in a brand new wooden fence, and from that time on, we couldn't keep her in the house. ***The instant that she felt protected she began to feel a freedom and liberty she hadn't felt before.***

Holiness should be viewed as God's protection for us. God has not placed us in a prison, but He has placed a protection around us to guard us against things that would harm us. If we allow the world in, it will destroy us; therefore, God has given us standards of holiness as a protective barrier to keep the world out.

For instance, God instructed us to save intimacy for marriage. Today we realize how much God protected us through this standard. By living inside God's barrier regarding intimacy, we are protected from disease, sadness, and having to raise children alone instead of with two parents.

God gave us standards for what we put into our bodies. Because we choose to live inside His barrier, we are protected from being addicted to alcohol or drugs.

We must learn that God has given us holiness not to imprison us, but to liberate us. When we see holiness as a protective boundary that God established to keep us from harm, we experience liberty and freedom. John 8:32 says it best, *"And ye shall know the truth, and the truth shall make you free."*

SIX

Principles

Unchangeable Laws

Principles are unchangeable laws that exist in the natural and the spiritual worlds. Gravity is a natural law or principle that determines the direction of moving objects within the earth's atmosphere. For example, apples fall to the ground; parachuters jump from airplanes and immediately begin to fall. The principle of gravity cannot be changed, but we have found ways to overcome the principle with great effort (e.g., airplanes and space shuttles). The plan of salvation is a basic principle or law that every person must obey to get into heaven. When a person is born again of the water and the Spirit (John 3:5), then that person has obeyed a spiritual principle; that person will receive the reward of heaven. The plan of salvation is a principle that is written in the Word of God and cannot be changed.

Subjection to Principles

Even before a person knows about the existence of a principle, he or she is subject to the power of that principle. Think about gravity. Even before Isaac Newton, sitting under the apple tree, realized the principle of gravity when the apple fell on his head, his body was subject to that principle. Isaac Newton had never floated off the ground, and if he had ever jumped off anything, his body had obeyed the law of gravity.

Even if a person doesn't know about the plan of salvation, he or she will still be subject to the principle at death. Hebrews 9:27 tells us that *"...it is appointed unto men once to die, but after this the judgment."* The verse doesn't point out any difference between those who obeyed the principle and those who did not. It says "unto men," meaning all people. So even if a person does not fully understand the principle, he or she will still be held accountable for the principle. Every person will still be under subjection to the principle's rules and rewards.

Mankind's Sinful Nature

To understand the importance of living by principle, a person must understand some basic facts concerning mankind. We are all born sinners. (Psalms 51:5, Romans 3:23) We have the nature of our father, Satan. (John 8:44) Even with the power of the Holy Ghost, it is difficult to overcome our sinful nature. (Romans 7:15-25)

First Step in Obtaining Holiness

We must first obtain salvation before we ever may obtain holiness. Every person must be born again. (John 3:3-5, Acts 2:38) A born again Christian will receive a new nature through the Holy Ghost. (II Peter 1:3, 4) With the Holy Ghost, a person has the ability to overcome sin. (Romans 6:6-7, 11-14, 17-18, 22)

Process of Holiness

Holiness means **conformity to the character of God**. It means to think as He thinks, love what He loves, hate what He hates, and act as Christ would act. (I Peter 1:15-16) Holiness is a process. (Hebrew 12:14) Moses and the children of Israel at Mt. Sinai were not all at the same level of holiness. God forbade the children of Israel to *touch* the mountain where the presence of God met with Moses. (Exodus 19:10-13) The Lord allowed Moses, Aaron, and the 70 elders to come a little further up the mountain. (Exodus 24:1, 9) Then Aaron and the elders had to stay at that point and God took Moses to the top of the mountain with Him. (Exodus 24:2, 15-18)

As Christians, we must have a certain tolerance for people who are in the process of holiness. We all are at different levels in our knowledge and understanding of God. We must trust that God and our pastor will determine those who stubbornly refuse to obey God's word.

Holiness is a continual process of sanctification (or cleansing). If a person does not continue in the process, that person will forfeit his or her born-again status. (Psalms 51:1-10)

Holiness is a two-part process: separation from this world or worldliness (II Corinthians 6:17) and dedication to God. (II Corinthians 6:18-17:1) *(2 Corinthians 6:18 - 7:1)*

Separation from Worldliness

The Bible offers examples of God's call for separation of His people from the world. Abram and his family had to separate from Ur of the Chaldees (Genesis 12:1-3); Abraham and Lot had to separate from each other (Genesis 13:8-13); and the children of Israel had to leave Egypt. (Leviticus 20:24-26)

God has always required that His people be something separate and set apart from everyone and everything else. John 15:19 says, *"...but because you are not of the world, but I have chosen you out of the world, therefore the world hateth you."* In Romans 12:1 He tells us to that we are not to "conform" to this world but to actually be transformed (completely different) than the world around us. True holiness will show its separation from the world. This does not mean that we look at what the world is doing and then do everything different just to be separate from them. What it means is that we live our lives according to the principles of the Word of God. And we don't allow the culture, the motives and the trends of the world to guide our lives. We don't change our beliefs because the world seems to be moving in a different direction. We have to learn how to balance our lives by living in this world but not just blindly adapting our beliefs to this ever-changing culture. This is why you must build your holiness on the principles of the Word of God.

If you read the entire book of Judges it is the story of a people struggling to maintain their separation from the worldly cultures around them. When the children of Israel lived their lives and guided their actions according to the commandments of God given to Moses, then they were blessed and prospered. But then they would get their eyes off the scriptures and look at the societies around them. They would begin to act, think, look and live like them. Each time, God removed His blessings from them and they begin to decline. The children of Israel would wind up in bondage and they would cry out to God and begin to repent and cleanse themselves. Then God would send them a deliverer or someone to help them defeat their enemies. Unfortunately, the cycle would begin all over again.

We must learn the lesson of the book of Judges. God separated His people for His glory. If we are truly going to be His people and His witness, then we are going to be different from the world around us.

Dedication to God

Separation from the world is essential for obtaining holiness, but it is not enough. God expects us to dedicate all of ourselves unto Him. Romans 12:1-2 tells us to present our bodies as a "living sacrifice." Remember that a living sacrifice can get off the altar, and that is why holiness is a continual dedication to God each day. Ephesians 4:22-24 encourages us to put off the things of the old man, and being renewed, take on the new man created in righteousness. God desires us to dedicate our lives continually unto Him.

It is not enough that we just separate from the world, that is only one-half of the equation. The problem with a lot of people in regarding holiness, is that work on only the separation part of the problem. They strive to be as different from the world as possible. But they do this more as an obligation unto God. His desire is that we not only be willing and have understanding regarding our need to be separate from the world, but that we also strive to dedicate our lives to Him.

Dedication to God is learning to love Him with all your heart. It is studying to show yourself approved by learning and understanding the principle and purpose behind holiness standards. Holiness was not designed to be lived only from a "separation" standpoint. God wants us to desire to do holiness because we have an understanding of the principle from the Word of God and a love in our hearts to be more like Him. This is what dedication unto God means.

The Lesson Of The Children Of Israel

To understand this concept of separation from the world and dedication to God, we have to look no further than the Children of Israel. God had sent them a Deliverer to lead them out (separation) from Egypt. Even though there was a temporary struggle for them to accomplish this – they did succeed. They came out of Egypt and even saw several victories along the way.

However, they found the dedication to God process so much more difficult. As they pursued separation there came a point where God desired more than just that – He desired them to dedicate (trust, follow). He wanted them to complete the mission He started in their lives. They were never intended to just run away from the world. And so they found themselves standing on the door of Canaan. This was the place where they could rest and develop a permanent, close relationship with God. But whereas coming out of Egypt was only slightly difficult, they found the dedication part of this process insurmountable. In fact the first time they found themselves here, they didn't succeed in completing the dedication part of this process. It would take 40 more years of running and separating from the world before they were ready to attempt dedication again.

We have to understand how important BOTH parts of this process are to God. Because without the separation from the world **AND** the dedication to God we have not completed true holiness.

Holiness means having no love in your heart for this world. God says that we are committing adultery against Him when we love the world more than Him. (James 4:4)

Holiness involves two parts of us: Inward Holiness—Spirit and Soul and Outward Holiness—Body. (I Corinthians 6:19-20; I Thessalonians 5:23; II Corinthians 7:1)

The Issue or the Principle

The reason that many Christians have trouble obeying the holiness standards long term is because they are focused on the issue and not the principle. They are consumed by how the issue is affecting them, versus being able to understand the need to obey the principle behind the issue. Each time that God demanded a holiness separation from His people, there was a spiritual principle behind it. **My greatest fear is that we are raising a generation that is trying to obey the issue without grasping the principle.** The principle is the foundation that will ground you when people question your actions, or when you have doubts, fears and frustrations.

The issue is the action or the outward standard that we obey. *But the issue is not the principle.* The scripture is clear on the subject of men and women's hair. Cutting or not cutting the hair is the issue but it is not the principle. The principle is submission to authority and what we do with our hair is just the evidence that we are in direct obedience or disobedience to the principle. I will share more regarding this specific principle later on in this book.

The issue is speaking with other tongues but that is not the principle. The principle is salvation and tongues is simply the outward evidence (standard) that we have obeyed the Biblical principle.

Don't get so consumed with the issues that you miss the principle. The principle is the foundation that we build our lives upon. The issue is simply the outward evidence that we have understood and obeyed the principle from the Word of God.

SEVEN

Standards

Christians develop personal standards for living when they dedicate their lives to God. Standards separate Christians from the world. Standards fall under two categories: inward holiness and outward holiness.

Inward Holiness

Standards for inward holiness include the way a person thinks and speaks and personal beliefs about where he or she may not go or things in which he or she may not participate, such as drugs, alcohol, pornography, gambling, etc. It also involves smaller inward acts of holiness such as guarding our tongues, keeping a right spirit, renewing our minds, and keeping unity among the brethren. Often, inward holiness is harder to maintain than outward holiness because these are things ingrained in our actions and character. This is where we must be completely "transformed" as Paul commands us in Romans 12:2.

Inward holiness issues are much easier to hide because the evidence of these do not always make themselves apparent in outward signs. If someone has difficulty in keeping a right spirit, you may not know that the first few times you are around them. But if you have prolonged exposure to these people, you will begin to see the signs of their inward condition. It is like cancer. You may have the disease for a while before you ever see any outward signs of your condition. But just like cancer, if inward holiness issues are not dealt with, then in time you will begin to see the outward destruction of the body.

Outward Holiness

Outward, or physical, standards pertain to a dress code and should reflect an inward holiness standard of modest.

Because holiness is a process and because Jesus tells us that it begins inwardly, more often than not, outward standards can take a while to manifest themselves in new converts. Just remember that this is process (remember Mt. Sinai) and you have to give time, teaching and the process of illumination for the new convert. However, outward holiness is also a sign of the condition of someone who has been walking with God for a while.

In using the example of the Shepherd, we see that the only way he knows that something is wrong with the sheep in his care is by their outward actions. If there is a sheep that is active, in the front of the fold, playing, eating well, and whose coat looks healthy, then the Shepherd knows that most likely that sheep is okay. However, if that same sheep all of the sudden is lethargic, not excited, straggling along behind the fold and with outward signs that they are sick, the Shepherd becomes concerned that something is wrong inwardly. So God does use our outward holiness standards (giving, dress, hair, worship, ministry, attendance) to let the Pastor know when someone is moving in the wrong direction. Remember the example I gave you previously about being a stumbling block for someone moving in the wrong direction. That is the Pastor's job in your life; to be your spiritual thermometer and let you know when you are moving in the wrong direction. Outward holiness is often the first signs that God gives a Pastor to know your spiritual condition.

The cause of Lucifer's fall began inwardly but then manifested itself outwardly (Ezekiel 28). Cain's outward countenance reflected his inward thought process (Genesis 4). We can never discount inward or outward holiness but realize that they work together as the evidence of our understanding of the principle behind the issue.

EIGHT

Living in Holiness

Now that we've seen that the order of holiness is vitally important to God, let's see how we should live. In Luke 6:36-45, Jesus tells us how we should live if we want to produce a holiness that will make us acceptable to Him and to His plan for our lives. He says, *"Be ye therefore **merciful**, as your Father also is **merciful. Judge not, and ye shall not be judged: condemn not, and ye shall not be condemned: forgive, and ye shall be forgiven:** For a good tree bringeth not forth corrupt fruit; neither doth a corrupt tree bring forth good fruit. For every tree is known by his own fruit. For of thorns men do not gather figs, nor of a bramble bush gather they grapes. A good man out of the good treasure of his heart bringeth forth that which is good; and an evil man out of the evil treasure of his heart bringeth forth that which is evil: **for of the abundance of the heart his mouth speaketh.**"*

Be Merciful!

If we are merciful, then God can also be merciful to us when we fail—not *if* we fail, but *when* we fail. We cannot be perfect. We will all be in need of mercy one day, so be sure to show mercy every day! In Matthew 5:7, Jesus tells us that merciful people are blessed because they can obtain mercy.

Don't Judge Others!

In Luke 6, Jesus tells us not to judge so that we won't be judged; not to condemn so that we won't be condemned; and to forgive so that we can be forgiven. We cannot receive blessings and goodness and longsuffering and understanding unless we are willing to give blessings and goodness and longsuffering and understanding. It is the principle of sowing and reaping again.

Plant the Right Seeds!

Just as we can sow and reap bad things, we can also sow and reap good things. But remember that whatever we sow WE WILL REAP AGAIN. In Luke 6:38-45, Jesus explains that trees produce what is in the seed. If we want God and others to be longsuffering with us, then we must return the favor. If we have seeds of judgment and condemnation in our hearts, then those things are definitely being produced by our mouths and lives. Remember that every time we speak, we are sowing seeds in the lives of the people around us. Whatever spirit or attitude we produce our children will also produce. People who say that everyone is always talking about them or their children should check their mouths and homes; they are probably reaping what they have sown. Jesus ended these words, *"...for of the abundance of the heart his mouth speaketh."* Look out mouth, you're telling on me!

NINE

Inward Holiness
What exactly is that?

Soul and Spirit

Inward holiness is allowing your "inward parts" (Psalm 51:6) to obey the Word of God and produce a change in your heart and mind. Inward holiness involves the spirit and soul. The **soul** is a person's mind, will, and emotions. The soul is driven by the five senses: touch, sight, smell, hearing, and seeing. The **spirit** is the part of a person that communicates with God.

From the beginning, we were designed that our soul and spirit would guide our actions. In the garden of Eden, Adam and Eve's actions were driven by their soul and spirit. Before they ate of the tree, each day their spirit was touched by the Spirit of God. Each day the Spirit of God would come down into the garden of Eden and His Spirit would communicate and touch the spirit of Adam and Eve. Then in turn, their spirit would control their soul, or their mind, will and emotion. The soul then in turn controlled the body. This is why after they had eaten of the tree of knowledge of good and evil, their spirit's actually died to the control of His Spirit. The whole story of the Bible is about God's search for a way to heal that breach so that His Spirit could lead and guide our actions.

A good example is if your hand touches a hot burner on the stove. First your spirit tells your mind, will and emotions that you are touching something hot. Then your emotions kick in because you actually feel the pain. This controls your action, which usually results in your quickly pulling your hand from the burner. All of this can happen in mere seconds but the process always remains the same.

This is why man has never been able to govern himself without laws and punishment. Our spirits are tainted and because of this it taints everything else in the downward line, our souls and our actions. You can see this in the progression of dispensations. When man tried to govern himself, following the cleansing of the earth after Noah, it wasn't too long before they were right back where they had started. We cannot govern ourselves without our spirit being touched by His Spirit and then allowing that Spirit to control our soul – our mind, will and emotions.

God's Desire

The rabbis' obsession with "ritual" purity led to neglect of inner spiritual purity.

In Psalm 51:6, David acknowledges God's desire for our lives. He says to the Lord, *"Behold, thou desirest truth in the **inward** parts...."* Why? God wants us to be inwardly holy because He is holy. In I Peter 1:16 God instructs us, *"Be ye holy; for I am holy."* A holy God cannot coexist with unrighteousness. With His Spirit guiding us we can become holy and live in holiness, being a "living sacrifice" that is "acceptable" to the Lord (Romans 12:1).

Don't do anything with your body that does not glorify God.

Inward Holiness before Outward Holiness

Holiness has an order to it, and it is three fold. Outward holiness without inward holiness is holiness that is in vain. Inward holiness must come before outward holiness.

Jesus told the Pharisees that they must clean up their spirits for their outward holiness to count towards righteousness. Jesus says in Matthew 23:26, *"Thou blind Pharisee, **cleanse first that which is within** the cup and platter, that the outside of them may be clean also."* Like the religious Pharisees, Christians often get the sequence of holiness backwards. This scripture shows that both inward and outward holiness are important to God; however, getting them in the right order is just as important.

In I Corinthians 6:20, the Apostle Paul commands Christians to *"glorify God in your body, **and in your spirit**."* We must make sure

Thought to have a double meaning with the Tyrian King + Satan.

that our inward actions are giving God true glory. Many times we glory in our outward holiness standards while inwardly we are ungodly. We must be careful or we can fall into the same trap Lucifer did as described in Ezekiel 28:12-18. In verse 15, Ezekiel writes, *"Thou wast perfect in thy ways from the day that thou wast created, **till iniquity was found in thee.**"* Lucifer was created to reflect the glory and holiness of God, but when he became consumed by his outward appearance of beauty and neglected his inward spirit, he fell. His sin began in the inward part of him and then contaminated the outward. Verse 17 states, *"Thine heart was lifted up because of thy beauty, thou hast corrupted thy wisdom by reason of thy brightness."* In I Thessalonians 5:23, Paul writes, *"...and I pray God your **whole spirit and soul** and body be preserved blameless unto the coming of our Lord Jesus Christ."* We have to be careful that we are not trying to uphold an outward holiness standard without striving for true inward change first.

Ezekial 28:17 is similar to the description for the serpent in Rev. 12:9.

The prayer for spirit and soul and body to be kept sound and blameless teaches that God sees the whole person as important in living a life pleasing to God.

TEN

Inward Holiness is Essential to Salvation

The Holy Ghost Makes Inward Holiness Possible

It is through the receiving of the Holy Ghost that we are able to have holiness in our inward parts. Remember we must have His Spirit cleansing our spirit so that we can really live a holy life.

Jeremiah 31:31-34 describes the new covenant between man and God, which was established on the day of Pentecost with the outpouring of the Holy Ghost. Acts 2:1-4 shows three steps to the initial infilling of the Holy Ghost: the Holy Ghost filled the house, it sat upon them, and, finally and most importantly, it FILLED them. God's Spirit wrote a new covenant on their hearts. From that day forward we have had the power of God *inwardly* to help us know Him and become like Him.

It's Up to You

While the Holy Ghost makes it possible for us to have inward holiness, it is still our responsibility to enact that power. In Proverbs 20:27, Solomon writes, "The *spirit of man* is the candle of the LORD, searching all the *inward* parts of the belly." Once our spirit has been revived by His Spirit, the Holy Ghost will send light into our lives and help us to clean up our inward man. John 3:21 states, "But he that doeth truth cometh to the light, that his deeds may be made manifest, that they are wrought in God." God will help us search and cleanse our inward parts, but first we must allow the Light of the World into our lives to change us.

Our outward appearance, the way we act, the way we look, and the way we speak will reveal what is within us. This is why it is important to make sure the inward part is cleansed and right in the eyes of God -- so that our outward actions can be made manifest. In Mark 7:14-23, Jesus teaches us that *"All these evil things come from within, and defile the man."* I would ask you, "With what are you filling the inward man?" The more you fill the inward part with the Spirit, the Word, and the Truth, the more you can produce holiness outwardly.

Inward Holiness is Essential for Salvation

Without holiness, we will not be saved (Hebrews 12:14). We must continually renew the Holy Ghost within us because without it we are unable to continue in holiness. Paul teaches in II Corinthians 4:16, "For which cause we faint not; but though our outward man perish, yet the *inward* man is renewed day by day." It is our responsibility to cleanse ourselves each day. Paul saw his need to die daily so that Christ could be glorified through him. God's mercy is new every morning, so all we need to do is ask His forgiveness and He will cleanse us.

ELEVEN

Inward Holiness Standards

Clean Heart, Right Spirit

II Corinthians 7:1 tells us to cleanse ourselves from all "filthiness of the spirit." Remember that a person's inward condition will produce outward fruits, so keeping a right spirit should be the first line of defense for a Christian. If your inward spirit is subjected to the Spirit of God, He will lead you and guide you into outward holiness. Many Christians have awesome outward holiness standards, but their inward parts are filthy in the sight of God. According to the Word of God, their holiness is in vain and eventually those inward sins are going to show up outwardly.

We may think that we know ourselves completely, but the Word shows us that there are things within us that we cannot even know or understand. We must make sure that we are cleansed from inward sins. Psalm 19:12 sets an example of prayer that we should follow: "Who can understand his errors? *cleanse thou me from secret faults.*" I want to make sure that I am right in God's sight, so daily repentance needs to be a part of my holiness process. Understanding that I will probably commit sins out of ignorance, I strive to make repentance a part of each prayer time.

David understood that sin started within, and he asked God to cleanse him from within. In Psalm 51:2, he prays, "Wash me thoroughly from mine iniquity, and cleanse me from my sin." Psalm 51:10: "*Create in me a clean heart, O God; and renew a right spirit within me.*" I firmly believe in praying the scripture, and this is one of my favorite passages to pray. I want God to be pleased with my life inwardly and outwardly, so I constantly ask Him to create His heart and Spirit within me.

God spoke through the prophet Ezekiel that the Holy Ghost would be given to mankind to cleanse us from our sin and give us the ability to have a right spirit (Ezekiel 36:24-27). Through the infilling of the Holy Ghost we have the ability to maintain a right spirit. In verse 27 God says, *"And I will put my spirit within you, and cause you to walk in my statutes, and ye shall keep my judgments, and do them."*

James 4:8 states, *"Draw nigh to God, and he will draw nigh to you. Cleanse your hands, ye sinners; and **purify your hearts,** ye double minded."* Remember that the reason for holiness is to be pleasing to God and accepted into His presence. He cannot dwell with sin, so we must purify our hearts and spirits to maintain His Spirit.

The way we cleanse our spirit is through repentance and the forgiveness of sins. *"But if we walk in the light, as he is in the light, we have fellowship one with another, **and the blood of Jesus Christ his Son cleanseth us from all sin.** If we say that we have no sin, we deceive ourselves, and the truth is not in us. If we confess our sins, he is faithful and just to forgive us our sins, **and to cleanse us from all unrighteousness."** (I John 1:7-9)* The way to keep a right spirit is to daily repent and cleanse ourselves from the ideology of this present world.

Renewed Mind

God spoke to Solomon concerning a "willing" or renewed mind in I Chronicles 28:9. He showed Solomon that the key to being accepted into His presence was knowing Him and seeking Him with a perfect heart and a willing (or renewed) mind. Our minds are where the battle for our souls begins, and when we are born again, we become a new creature in Christ. However, the battle for our minds continues daily. Satan uses every tool he has available to win this battle, so it takes an effort and agreement with God to stay in a renewed mind on a daily basis.

Pastors and teachers must understand that our job is to change minds, not hearts. Only God can change a heart, but we must continually teach the Word of God so that knowledge can increase. Teaching the Word of God instills truth in the minds of the students, and their hearts are sure to follow. Many times we try to change hearts, which people may resist because they don't have a foundation of knowledge on which to base the change in their lives.

A renewed mind brings peace to a life. In Isaiah 26:3, the prophet states, *"Thou wilt keep him in perfect peace, whose **mind** is stayed on thee: because he trusteth in thee."* If a person's mind is renewed in Christ, that person will produce peace personally and then peace in the home and peace in the church. Many churches suffer continually with church problems because the church members do not have renewed minds; they are carnally minded. Romans 8:6-7 states, "For to be carnally minded is death; but to be *spiritually minded is life and peace.* Because the carnal **mind** is enmity against God: for it is not subject to the law of God, neither indeed can be." We must keep our minds centered on God and His Word and be filled with His Spirit. If we do our part, He has promised us life and peace.

Jesus said that the greatest commandment of all is for a person to love God with all his or her mind (Matthew 22:37). There is a saying that if you live for God easy, it is hard; but if you live for God hard, it is easy. We must make sure that our minds are committed to Christ first, and then our bodies will follow. When you love God with everything you are, then there is no room left over to give to other things. Christ-centered lives are truly holy lives.

Paul shows us that we can renew our mind and bring it into captivity to serve the law of God. Romans 7:25: *"I thank God through Jesus Christ our Lord. So then with the **mind** I myself serve the law of God; but with the flesh the law of sin."* If we give our flesh free reign, it will always serve itself first. That is why a person must "make up his mind" to serve God. Filling your mind with the Word of God by reading, memorizing, and meditating on the scripture is teaching your flesh to serve God every day.

You can be transformed by the renewing of your mind! The very root of holiness is transformation of both mind and body to be like

Christ. In Romans 12:2 we see that the transformation begins with a renewed mind. Reading the Word of God shows us how to live, praying helps us to agree with God, and walking in the Spirit produces holiness in our lives. Once the battle for your mind is won, you can then begin living a new life of righteousness and "true" holiness according to Ephesians 4:23-24.

We must have a renewed mind so that we may have the mind of Christ. I Corinthians 2:16: "For who hath known the mind of the Lord, that he may instruct him? But we have the **mind** of Christ." Philippians 2:5: "Let this *mind* be in you, which was also in Christ Jesus." Pray to have the mind of God. If we put on His mind, then we know we are on the path to holiness.

Shun the Works of the Flesh

We must work hard every day to shun the works of the flesh as described in Galatians 5:19-21. Many people say they would never be an adulterer, a fornicator, involved in witchcraft or drunken; however, we sometimes overlook the smaller works of the flesh. Many times we are foolish in our behavior, constantly in variance or conflict with one another, or don't want to be submitted to authority in our lives, emulating the stature of pastor or teacher. I think we must take another look at this scripture and make sure that our outward holiness is reflecting a true inward holiness.

The following are definitions of the works of the flesh noted in Galatians 5:19-21: "uncleaness" is being immoral or indecent; "lasciviousness" is having vices; "variance" is having conflict; "emulations" is to try to be equal (Satan's sin was that he tried to be equal to God); "seditions" is to cause discord; "heresies" is to cause confusion from the truth or embracing false doctrine; and "revelries" is foolishness or carousing.

Jesus lets us know that all these outward signs start inwardly. He says in Matthew 5:28, *"But I say unto you, That whosoever looketh on a woman to lust after her hath committed adultery with her already in his heart."* In I John 3:15, He says, "Whosoever **hateth his** *brother is a murderer....*" Many people say that living under the Old Testament law would have been easier, but Jesus dispels that notion in the scriptures above. In the Old Testament you had to be found in the act of adultery to be punished, and you had to have actually killed someone to be a murderer. In the New Testament, Jesus shows us that the mind is where the sin begins. If you lust after a woman (an inward thought), in His eyes you have already committed adultery. If you hate your brother (an inward emotion), you have already committed murder in God's eyes. This scripture shows us the importance of keeping an inwardly clean spirit, mind, and heart so that we can be holy in God's sight.

Guard Your Tongue

A large part of holiness is guarding the tongue. When we allow our tongue to control us, then we will always wind up in trouble. It is hard work for a person to guard his tongue, but until a person can control it, that person cannot live in true holiness.

We are instructed in Psalm 34:13 to **"Keep thy tongue from evil,** *and thy lips from speaking guile."* This scripture lets you know it is *your* responsibility to control your tongue. It says, *"Keep thy"*! Your job is to control what comes out of your mouth.

I Peter 3:10 states, *"For he that will love life, and see good days, let him* **refrain his tongue from evil,** *and his lips that they speak no guile...."* If you want peace and happiness, you will learn early on to control what comes from your mouth. I have a personal mantra: If you know someone is talking about me, DON'T TELL ME! If I know, then I will have to pray through it and forgive them. I want a life of peace and joy and I want to greet my brothers and sisters without any restraint from my heart, so I do two things: I watch what I say, and I don't listen to negative talk from others.

Proverbs 18:21 states, **"Death and life are in the power of the tongue**: *and they that love it shall eat the fruit thereof."* If you find someone who loves to "talk" about others, AVOID THIS PERSON! If you learn to love the taste of that fruit you will find that one day you have to eat it also! You have the power to build someone up or to destroy someone by what you say. The best advice is to keep your mouth shut and let God take care of the situation. Remember He will guard your back and if you are right you don't need to defend yourself.

 James 1:26 teaches us, *"If any man among you seem to be religious, and **bridleth not his tongue**, but deceiveth his own heart, this man's religion is vain."* Don't be deceived; just because everyone *attends* church doesn't mean they are *in* church. Don't be too upset when your "brothers" talk about you; remember that some people's religion is vain, according to the Word of God. You can tell these people by the ones who can't control their tongues.

*"Even so the tongue is a little member, and boasteth great things. Behold, how great a matter a little fire kindleth! **And the tongue is a fire, a world of iniquity: so is the tongue among our members, that it defileth the whole body,** and setteth on fire the course of nature; and it is set on fire of hell…. But the **tongue can no man tame; it is an unruly evil, full of deadly poison."** (James 3:5-6, 8)* We must realize that our tongues are evil and the only way to keep them under control is to subject them to Spirit of God. If you are using your mouth to praise God you shouldn't have time to destroy others. You must understand your role for the Pastor is to be a fireman, not an arsonist! When you are a part of a conversation that is not right, you can either pour water or gasoline on it. Your pastor needs you to pour out water and put out those fires before they get out of control. By learning to separate yourself from people who talk, you will find they don't come to you anymore and this will bring great joy and peace to your life.

Abstain from the Appearance of Evil

I Thessalonians 5:22 admonishes us to *"**Abstain from all appearance of evil.** And the very God of peace sanctify you wholly; and I pray God your **whole spirit and soul** and body be preserved blameless unto the coming of our Lord Jesus Christ."* There are many things I could participate in that wouldn't be sin; but I don't want to ruin my witness. The Lord asks us to abstain from all appearance of evil. That means that many things we choose not to do just because we want to be a true witness of God. We want to "preserve" ourselves in holiness that we may be acceptable to God.

TWELVE

Fruits of Inward Holiness

Fruits of the Spirit

It's not enough to just shun the works of the flesh, guarding your tongue, and avoiding the appearance of evil. You must be actively producing the fruit of the Spirit described in Galatians 5:22-24. I have often asked people, "What are you promoting in your church?" Is it love, joy, and peace? Are you longsuffering towards your brothers and sisters? Are you meek? Do you produce faith? Many people will tell you they don't sin by committing the works of the flesh, but they also are not producing inward holiness through the fruit of the Spirit.

Paul says in Ephesians 5:9-10, "(For the **fruit** of the Spirit is in all goodness and righteousness and truth;) ***Proving what is acceptable unto the Lord***." Remember holiness is about being acceptable to God, and this scripture lets us know that producing the fruit of the Spirit is one step in the right direction.

Unity & Love for One Another

One of the greatest witnesses of holiness is unity among the brethren. And yet, unity is one of the greatest problems in our local churches. We say we are Christians, yet we devour one another. Many Christians need to take a moment and look within themselves and really gain a love for one another. (Read I Thessalonians 3:12-13; 4:6-9, I John 3:11-23, and I John 4:7-12, 20-21)

John 13:34-35 shows us that the only way the world knows we belong to Christ is our love for one another -- not our love for Him necessarily, but how we treat each other. A large part of holiness is creating unity in our churches by loving, caring, praying, and ministering to one another.

There is no greater love manifested, in the eyes of God, than a person loving his or her neighbor. In John 15:12-13, Jesus tells us that we truly know love when we are willing to deny ourselves, or "die" to the flesh, so that someone else can be saved. Sometimes we are talked about, mistreated, and abused by the very people who are supposed to support us in love; however, a true, holy Christian is one who sees the greater purpose in the Kingdom of God and holds his tongue. Remember that God said He rewards all vengeance (Romans 12:19). We need to withhold our personal issues and love one another so that unity will not be destroyed.

Many people think that loving one another is a choice, but Christ "commands" us to love one another. He says, *"These things I command you, that ye* **love one another.***"* (John 15:17) This is your scripture for those people who are often difficult to love; just remember that Christ commands us to love one another.

You will know that you have true unity in love when you are unselfish in your dealings with your spiritual brethren. Paul reminds us in Romans 12:10 to *"Be kindly affectioned one to another with* **brotherly love***; in honour preferring one another...."*

In II Corinthians 2:4 – 8, Paul wants the church to understand that when we are "grieved," or wronged, by someone, instead of retaliating, God wants us to forgive and restore this person so that the enemy cannot swallow them up.

Many people use the liberty that we feel in the Spirit to abuse one another. In Galatians 5:13-14 we see that if we abuse the liberty that God gave us, we become spiritual cannibals. I have been to many churches where on the surface they appeared (in dress) to be in agreement with holiness, but there was an undertow of envy, jealousy, and bitterness. People were talking about and against each other. They were biting and devouring one another. Paul said if you allow this to continue in your church, eventually everyone will be consumed. We must guard our churches and especially our new converts, so that they enter a place of love, not destruction.

Unity comes through love. Ephesians 4:2-3 states: "With all lowliness and meekness, with longsuffering, forbearing one another in **love**; Endeavoring to keep the unity of the Spirit in the bond of peace." Love will produce unity. When everyone knows they are loved, they will be more inclined to work together for the Kingdom.

Colossians 2:2 talks about being "knit together in love." When you look at a knitted fabric, you see that it would be very difficult to tear it apart. To destroy a knitted garment you either unravel it from the beginning or cut it. You cannot break a knitted garment. If we can knit ourselves together with love, then it will be very hard to tear us apart. And the beauty of a knitted garment is that the more you knit, the stronger it grows. The more we love and include people in our church, the harder it is to break our unity.

Outward Holiness

Inward Holiness is the second step in the process of holiness. After we achieve the right attitude and understand the underlying principles for holiness, we are to begin to apply those to our bodies. Jesus clearly tells the Pharisees to clean up their inward parts or their outward holiness is in vain. Remember that inward holiness produces outward fruit. I must be striving each day of my life to keep a right spirit, to renew my mind from carnality to spirituality, to actively produce the fruit of the spirit, not just shunning the works of the flesh, and to guard my tongue and my witness. God desires truth in our inward parts, and it is our responsibility to maintain not only our outward man but our inward man as well.

Heavenly Reward

In Hebrews 12:14, Paul says, "Follow peace with all men, and holiness, **_without which no man shall see the Lord._**" In the process of "following" Christ, our reward at the end of this life is to see the

Lord and be in His presence. Many people allow the standards of holiness to block their view of the reward of holiness. Remember that we don't live for this present world, but for the world to come. Holiness is our ticket into the presence of God.

THIRTEEN

Outward Holiness

Outward after *Inward*

Holiness has an order, and it must be obeyed in that order. First, we must have the right attitude concerning holiness. Having the right attitude throughout the process of holiness will be the key to our outward holiness being acceptable in the sight of God. Once we have the correct attitude, we must then understand the principles of holiness laid out in the Word of God. The principles help us to understand why holiness is important to God, and they give us guidelines to help us when we face issues of holiness in modern times. Living by principles based on the Word of God is a very safe and protected position.

After obtaining a right attitude and gaining an understanding of God's principles, we can begin to develop standards of holiness in our lives. Inward holiness must be present before true outward holiness can be attained. Inward holiness is keeping a right spirit, a renewed mind, a guarded tongue, and having love for and unity with one another. These things are matters of the inward man, and God desires that our inward parts be holy before Him.

What God Sees

The final step of holiness is our outward appearance. Many people want to misuse the scripture in I Samuel 16:7 that says "for the LORD seeth not as man seeth; for man looketh on the outward appearance, but the LORD looketh on the heart" to mean that God is not concerned with our outward appearance. The setting of this scripture is Samuel's mission to anoint a new king in Israel. His eye was caught by the beauty of Eliab, the son of Jesse, and he assumed that Eliab was surely the anointed of the Lord. That is when the Lord made Samuel aware that He was looking for different qualifications in the next king of Israel.

God *is* concerned with our outward appearance. Our outward appearance is a separation from the world, and it is our witness of the inward change God has made in our lives when He fills us with His Spirit. The Lord shows us the importance of outward holiness in Matthew 23:25-26 when He criticizes the religious leaders of the day: *"Woe unto you, scribes and Pharisees, hypocrites! for ye make clean the outside of the cup and of the platter, but within they are full of extortion and excess. Thou blind Pharisee, cleanse first that which is within the cup and platter, **that the outside of them may be clean also.**"* Yes, the condition of the inside of a person is very important to God, but Jesus lets us know that inward holiness is what helps us clean up our outside appearance. We wouldn't wash the inside of a plate and cup without taking time to make sure the outside was clean also. We must make sure that our outward man is involved in the process of holiness along with our inward man.

A Nightstick, a Measuring Stick, and a Walking Stick

During my research and prayer concerning this subject I felt the Lord gave me an analogy between holiness and sticks. We use holiness as three different sticks -- a nightstick, a measuring stick, and walking stick.

A nightstick is used primarily for law enforcement. Police officers use it to subdue or beat down someone who is committing an offense. As Christians, we often use holiness as a nightstick to force people to submit to our beliefs. A nightstick is never viewed in a positive manner by its victim. It is simply a tool to inflict pain and keep a person in line with a set of rules.

A measuring stick is only as good as the measurement you assign. The only person who knows the measurement is the person with the stick. Many times we use outward holiness as a measuring stick. If someone doesn't measure up to our expectations, or measurements, then they are not holy in our sight. Jesus told us to first get the beam from our eye before working on the splinter in someone else's (Luke 6:41-42). He was telling us to be careful about pulling out our holiness measuring sticks and using them on each other.

The purpose of a walking stick is to help balance a person. This is the kind of holiness we need to emulate and strive to produce. Holiness in our lives is to bring balance so that we can please God and be accepted into His presence. A walking stick can only benefit someone else if the person with the stick has balance. We cannot help someone else produce holiness unless we are first following the entire process of holiness. I want to have a walking stick holiness so that it can produce balance in my life and then I, in turn, can help others find balance in their lives.

A Godly Principle Passed Down

One of my greatest concerns is when I hear this upcoming generation say that they don't believe that some of the outward holiness standards, that we have held fast to for so many years, are "important" anymore. I am not blind to the fact that culture is different and that perhaps there are a few things that due to the advancement of this age have morphed overtime to reflect more modernization. However, those always need to be weighed against the underlying principle from the Word of God before changing. And example of this might be regarding the topic of television. Many years ago TV was a unit in your home with rabbit ears that brought in no more than 4 channels. So we could preach against having these in our homes and allowing them to steal our time and distract our attention from God. However, due to the advent of so much technology we have had to adjust our viewpoint because now the box is not just in a home, but most people carry access to this on their cellphones or tablets. So preaching against the "box" is not wise nor does it maintain the underlying Biblical principle that we need to be teaching. The principle is that we "make a covenant with our eyes" as Job stated and not "put any wicked thing before our eyes". If we live our lives by this principle then it doesn't matter where the box is – we will always make sure we are being obedient to outward holiness in our lives. So I strongly push basing all your outward holiness standards on Biblical principles that surpass time and culture.

With that said, I do feel that this generation has to be extremely careful that we are not using culture to move us away from the principles of the Word of God. In the Old Testament we see the story of Moses at the burning bush. Exodus 3:3-5 relates this story but I am drawn to verse 5, *"And he said, Draw not nigh hither: put off thy shoes from off thy feet; for the place whereon thou standest is holy ground."* God began right at this moment to teach Moses a lesson regarding holiness, standards and His presence. Remember in earlier chapters I told you that holiness is all about access to the presence of God. The more of this world that you put off the more access to God's presence you can experience. The mount Sinai example used earlier in this book explains this concept. Moses could ascend to the top of the mountain because he had learned the principle of putting off something to have more access to the presence of God. He learned that here in Exodus 3. God showed Moses that outward holiness is important to Him because God chose an item of clothing for Moses to remove as a symbol that he was willing to be cleansed so that he could approach God.

Then came the day that Moses passed off the scene and the next pastor stepped up. God anointed Joshua to become the leader and pastor of Israel. Joshua is ready to begin the greatest period of revival and growth for Israel. But before this takes place God wants to be sure that the new generation *still lives* by the principle established in the previous generation. In Joshua 5:13-15 we see the story of Joshua standing at the precipice of his greatest victory – Jericho. He lifts up his eyes and sees a man standing with a sword drawn. Joshua walks over to him and asks, "Art thou for us, or for our adversaries?" The angel responds by basically saying, "Neither, I'm on the Lord's side". What a reflection of holiness because holiness is NOT ABOUT YOU – it is about His Kingdom, His Presence and His Power.

In verse 15 God speaks to Joshua and asks him to do something. *"Loose thy shoe from off thy foot; for the place whereon thou standest is holy."* Almost the exact same wording that God shared with the previous pastor, Moses. God is showing us that even though there may be a new leader, a new territory to claim, a new level to reach – the way into His presence will NEVER CHANGE! You have to make sure that you still know the formula to have access to His presence.

This is my greatest concern when I see men and women around me that have been raised under the "burning bush" principle of holiness and access to God. But then I see them begin to move away stating that they don't "feel" or "think" that this is important any more. When I look back at two of the greatest leaders of the Bible – Moses & Joshua – they each lead at different times, different eras, gained different territory and worked with different people but they lived under the same principle of the purpose and vision of holiness – access to God!

Perspectives

To truly understand and explain outward holiness in this day and age, we have to look at it from three perspectives.

First, what does the Bible teach concerning the issue? The Bible is our foundation of beliefs, and it's very important that we are able to back things up with the Word of God. During my days in Bible school, a theology teacher explained it this way: where the Bible speaks, you speak; where the Bible is silent, you be silent. We must have the Word to back up our beliefs.

Second, we must look at history. We must understand how our culture has changed, particularly in the past decade. What were the motivating factors that cause us to believe certain things are okay today when a little over 100 years ago they were wrong? We have to dig below the surface to see how our worldly culture has affected our standards of holiness.

Third, we must take principles found in the Scripture and our culture's history into account when making up a standard for living holy in modern times.

We'll look at several areas of holiness using these perspectives in this study. I trust that when you have finished this booklet, you will have a better understanding and a deeper appreciation for dedicating yourself to God through outward holiness.

FOURTEEN

Why Standards

Wordless Conversations

Our outward appearance is not only a reflection of our inward condition, but it also identifies who we are. When we walk through the mall, we have a conversation with everyone we pass, and we never say a word! What you wear says something about who you are and what you believe in. The world acknowledges this fact by placing certain people into easily identifiable uniforms. For instance, policemen, firefighters, doctors, athletic teams, prisoners, etc. wear clothes that identify them as such. Even though the world wants to tell us that we can be independent in our dress, their actions say something else entirely. We identify people and pass judgment on their beliefs according to their outward appearance.

Modest Apparel

In Genesis 38 the Bible tells a story of a woman who deceived her father-in-law simply by changing her manner of dress. The story shows us that even then people were identified by the way they dressed. Judah thought that his own daughter-in-law, Tamar, was a prostitute simply by how she was dressed. "When Judah saw her, he thought her to be an harlot; because she had covered her face" (verse 15). Proverbs 7:10 also mentions the "attire of an harlot." We cannot say that what we wear is not important when even the world identifies it as important.

In I Timothy 2:9-10 the scriptures says, "In like manner also, that women adorn themselves in modest apparel, with shamefacedness and sobriety; not with broided hair, or gold, or pearls, or costly array; But (which becometh women professing godliness) with good works." The word "modest" here is the Greek word *kosmios*, which means well orderly and proper. How we dress and behave says a lot about who we are as women. We profess godliness (or that we are trying to be like Him), yet our appearance denies the fact that we are His. We must understand that what we wear identifies whom we belong to. Genesis 1:27 says, "So God created man in his own image in the image of God he created him; male and female he created them." We were created to reflect the image of God. The way that He created us is the way that He desires to see us. There is distinction in dress and gender. Genesis specifically tells us that we were created beautiful and that there is a difference between male and female. We are identified as His by the way we adorn ourselves outwardly.

Principle Versus Positional Standards

Earlier in this book, we discussed the importance of principles. And we understand that there are many areas in which the Bible is extremely clear that this is not a suggestion but rather a commandment with a principle attached to it. The same applies in the Christian Discipleship area of holiness. There are certain holiness standards, which have a very clear and defined spiritual principle attached to them. And as we are obedient to these standards we release the principle in our lives.

But there are some holiness standards that do not have a clear, defined spiritual principle attached to them. Rather, as we study these standards throughout the Bible, we see them as positional standards. In other words, as people moved their position closer to God, they applied these standards to their lives. When they moved away from God, they would go back and pick up these things. This is why we call these *positional* standards.

When looking at the standards found in the Word of God, we see that there are two that have very clear defined spiritual principles applied to them; clothing and hair. When we obey in these areas we release the blessing of the spiritual principle. When we disobey we also release the curse of the spiritual principle in our lives.

There are other standards that the Word does not have a clear, defined spiritual principle applied to them. But as you read the Biblical accounts of them, you realize that these were positional standards. When God desired His people to be closer to Him, He would request them to remove these items. When the people would grow cold in the Lord, they would go back and pick up these items. So even though there is not a direct, clear spiritual principle applied to these standards, it does not mean they are not important. They show, outwardly, the condition of our spiritual relationship and commitment to God. They show our **position** with Him.

The Goose & The Gander

You know that old saying, "What's good for the goose is good for the gander". Basically saying that men and women both must do the same thing. In the Apostolic world, however, I have often heard the comment that there seems to be a lot of standards for women and not as many for men. I disagree with this. As you read through the standards in the next few chapters, you will see that every one of them is to be applied in obedience in both genders. There may be a different application but there should be the same obedience to the principles and positional standards asked of us by God.

When we talked about spiritual principles above we noted that there were two standards that had definite spiritual principles applied to them; clothing and hair. These are the same for both men and women – but in different applications. This means that there is a standard for clothing and hair for men and women. They are each expected to participate in the standard so that the spiritual principle will be applied and the attached blessing or curse will be released in their lives.

FIFTEEN

Separation By Clothing

The Biblical Perspective

To understand the spiritual principle of clothing, you have to travel all the way back to the Garden of Eden. Genesis 1:27, *"So God created man in his own image, in the image of God created he him; **male and female created he them.**"* Immediately, we see a spiritual principle born, there will be two distinct gender roles and these roles will be defined in everything; in their bodies, in how they dress and in their purpose.

The spiritual principle behind our clothing is that we maintain a distinction between men and women. When we look at the actions of the world in changing how men and women dress, we can step back and see the spiritual principle motivating all this change. Satan does not have original ideas of his own. His only purpose is to present his *twist* on the ideas (commandments) of God. And the only thing he can do is get us to agree to cross gender lines in our dress and then he gets us to disobey the spiritual principle. When you see the spiritual principle attached and you understand the tactics of the enemy, you can then look beyond culture and the influence of the fashion industry. They are simply carrying out the wishes of the enemy without truly understanding the spiritual principle behind their actions.

Even the world subconsciously admits that there is a spiritual principle attached to this standard. They do things without even realizing that the DNA that God created in them is making this choice. Every bathroom door across America has two symbols, one representing male and one representing female. The male symbol is a man in pants; the female symbol is a woman wearing a triangular skirt. So even in America they still define women and men by clothing. And they define men's clothing as trousers or pants and women's clothing as a skirt.

We see this continued when we study the homosexual world. Whenever you see them together, one will take on the masculine role and one will take on the feminine role. If homosexuality is just about being able to love someone, then why do they go back and adapt to the original gender roles? Because it is a spiritual principle created into their DNA, and no matter how they try and bypass the letter of the law they will never be able to change the spirit of the principle. Their heart and spirit will always try and recreate these roles, because it tells them that this is innately correct. No matter the action, the spiritual principle shines through.

In Deuteronomy 22:5 the Lord shares His desire for the sexes to remain separate in dress by saying, *"The woman shall not wear that which pertaineth unto a man, neither shall a man put on a woman's garment: for all that do so are abomination unto the LORD thy God."* The key to understanding this verse is the word "pertaineth." Many people today want to tell us that there are "women's" pants or other items that are specifically made for women. But the Lord said it this way so that we could realize that once again He is stressing the distinction of the sexes. In our culture there is one item of clothing that is strictly male and that is pants or trousers. The only type of man who would wear a dress in our culture is a transvestite. Ordinary men would never dream of putting on a dress or skirt. So we can say that any type of pants is an item of clothing pertaining to a man. God asked women to abstain from wearing those garments, which pertain to the male gender so that we can be distinctive in our dress. Remember that holiness is about being pleasing to God. The last part of this verse tells us that when we don't dress distinctively according to our sex, we actually become an abomination in His sight. I have often asked people how they feel when they see a male transvestite. I know that I am completely disgusted or become almost sick to my stomach to see that kind of perversion. But the scripture plainly tells us that God views a woman who dresses as a man in the same way. They make Him sick to His stomach. We don't need to justify the way we dress; we just need to obey the Word of God and remain female in our dress.

One of the most powerful scriptures in the Bible concerning holiness is found in Romans 12:1-2. *"I beseech you therefore, brethren, by the mercies of God, that ye present your bodies a living sacrifice, holy, acceptable unto God, which is your reasonable service. And be not conformed to this world: but be ye transformed by the renewing of your mind, that ye may prove what is that good, and acceptable, and perfect, will of God."* The scripture clearly states that we must present our entire bodies unto the Lord as holy. It cannot only be our inward parts, but it must be our outward appearance as well. In verse 2, Paul tells us that we are to be "transformed," not "conformed," to this world. When a person becomes a Christian, he or she should not conform to the standards of this world which tell us how to live, how to dress, and how to look. We should be transformed completely. To be transformed is to be completely changed! To do a 180-degree turn and change who we are. Many people "accept Christ," but they are never inwardly or outwardly transformed. When you really become a Christian, you will change in your outward appearance as well as your inward appearance.

Our Culture's Perspective

Even our culture acknowledges the distinction between male and female. The definition of the word "trousers" in the dictionary shows that the garment is distinctively men's clothing. It is defined in Webster's Revised Unabridged Dictionary (©1996, 1998 MICRA, Inc.) as "a garment worn by men and boys, extending from the waist to the knee or to the ankle, and covering each leg separately." Many people want to say that pants or trousers are female clothing, but culturally and by definition, they are men's clothing.

We even use phrases to denote the fact that pants are a sign of gender and authority. We ask, "Who wears the pants in that family?" We associate pants with the male or leadership role in the family. We cannot say that clothing doesn't define what gender role we are trying to play.

The Historical Perspective

If you need anymore convincing, let's look at the history of trousers. How did we get to the point where pants are an acceptable piece of clothing for women? What were the influencing factors in this change in culture? Remember that Paul tells us in Romans to be transformed or changed, not to conform to the culture around us.

The idea of wearing split pants came directly from the Women's Liberation Movement. The women who started this movement were all extremely liberal in their thinking and very opposed to submission to men or to the Bible. In the 1700's the leader of the movement was Mary Wollstonecraft. She wrote a book entitled, *A Vindication of the Rights of Woman* in 1792. She rebelled against all the moral and decent laws of that day, even living with a man and giving birth to a child out of wedlock. Then in the 1800's, two women stepped forward to try to push the women's movement even farther. Lucretia Mott and Elizabeth Cady Stanton were both greatly opposed to the Bible, especially on the subject of divorce. In fact, Elizabeth Cady Stanton wrote a paper in which she says, "I rejoice over every slave that escapes from a discordant marriage." On July 19, 1848, the first Women's Rights Convention was held in Seneca Falls, New York. It was only two years later, in 1850, that women began to wear trousers (at that time called bloomers) underneath shortened dresses.

Amelia Bloomer, a feminist editor, was the first to start this trend, thus the name "bloomers." Even Ms. Bloomer in her magazine, *The Lily*, said in 1851 that she hoped "female readers will not be shocked by her appearance or that her male readers would not mistake her for a man." This was quoted beneath a cartoon rendering of her in her "bloomers." What the power of the printed word could not do, the power of the visual aid could. Amelia Bloomer could not change the course of history just through a few cartoon drawings, but with the advent of the movie industry in the 1920's, our culture took a dramatic turn.

In the 1920's, three things took place that began our blurring of the gender lines. First was World Wars I and II. Men went to war and women had to step into their jobs. As women began to take on more and more of the male role in society, their dress began to change as well. Second was a renewal of the Women's Rights Movement that took place around that time. Women began to realize that if they were going to take on the men's responsibilities in the workplace, they wanted the men's rights as well. Last was advent of the movie industry.

One of the greatest influential figures of the 1920's and 1930's was an actress by the name of Marlene Dietrich. She was a self-proclaimed bi-sexual and her favorite item to wear was a man's double-breasted pant suit. She was also one of the most famous actresses of that day. Once America began this diet of war, women's rights, and movies, it wasn't long until they began imitating what they were seeing. In 1939, women began to openly wear slacks. In January 1955 the state of California passed a law giving women the right to wear trousers to work.

From the advent of the movie industry in the 1920's, we can see the rapid downward progression of clothing. In 1925 short skirts began to appear. For the first time a woman would show her ankle and calf -- something that had never been done before. In 1939 women began to wear slacks. In 1960 we were introduced to the miniskirt, pants suits, hot pants, and short shorts. The designers of the 1960's said they were striving to make "uni-sex" clothing -- in other words, clothing that could be worn by either sex. Through the next decades we have seen clothing drastically change. Today clothing has been so gender-blurred that it is hard to tell a man from a woman many times.

As women have taken the male gender roles, men have stepped back into the female gender roles. Men today wear earrings, they grow their hair long, and they wear multiple rings and necklaces.

Often times it is hard to determine the gender of people when their backs are turned to us.

We must be careful that we are pleasing to God in our dress. Not only must we dress in the gender role that He created us in, but we must be careful to maintain our modesty in our clothing. I once heard it asked, "If Jesus walked into the room would you be comfortable dressed as you are?" This is a question that we need to ask ourselves each time we get dressed. God desires us to remain in the role He created for us and to be careful that we glorify Him in our dress.

Here is a summary of our standard of dress through the biblical and historical perspectives. In Genesis 1:27, God set up a principle. He created us to maintain our distinction as male and female. He commands us in Deuteronomy 22:5 to make sure that we are dressing based on our gender. The apostle Paul tells us in I Timothy 2:9 to dress modestly to be pleasing to God. Historically, our concept of what is acceptable for a man to wear and for a woman to wear has been influenced by ungodly groups and social movements. The truth of the matter has not changed; our culture still uses pants to identify males and skirts to identify women. We must conclude that women should abstain from wearing pants just as men should abstain from wearing skirts or dresses.

God tells us in I Peter to be holy because He is holy. We cannot follow after movies, the Women's Rights Movement, and other things that are not of God. These are Satan's tools to distract us and make our lives not pleasing unto God. We must develop a love for God and His ways so that we can overcome the world and its pressures.

SIXTEEN

Separation By Hair

The Biblical Perspective

First we must establish what the entire concept of hair is about. It is not simply about having long hair on a woman or short hair on a man, but it is actually about a very important concept from the Bible — submission to authority. That is why the entire scripture setting for the discussion on hair begins with Paul saying in I Corinthians 11:3, *"But I would have you know, that the head of every man is Christ, and the head of the woman is the man; and the head of Christ is God."* Paul is very clear at the beginning of the issue concerning hair that this is about submission to the chain of authority established by God. When a woman remains in submission to her head, the man, there are blessings and protection that follows. You will see later on when we discuss the history of hair that the movement came out of a spirit of rebellion. Women did not want to remain in their God-ordained position and so began the process of cutting that authority. Many women will say that when they cut their hair they feel that they have been freed from a bondage that they felt in before. Do I believe that they really feel a spirit of freedom? Yes! But it is a spiritual feeling, not just an emotional or physical feeling. When they cut their hair, they actually step out of their role as a woman and into the man's position of authority. Of course our flesh loves this feeling. It is the same feeling that Satan wanted when he desired to step out of submission to authority in heaven. Isaiah 14:12-15 describes how Satan desired to be lifted up and become equal to God. In Galatians 5:19, we see the works of the flesh being laid out. In Galatians 5:20 we see one of the works of the flesh is "emulations," which means "to be equal to." That was the spirit that Satan exhibited in Isaiah when he desired to be equal to God. That is the same spirit that will come upon us when we step out of our specified role in submission to authority.

Not only is the condition of our hair a sign of our submission to authority, but it also places us once again in obedience to Genesis 1:27 where the Lord created us distinctly male and female. As we look through I Corinthians 11 we will see that our hair defines us our physical role as well. There are basic laws in nature that define what is male and what is female.

Paul's instructions on hair begin with the order that God created for authority. The man is the head of the woman, and as such he must be in his place of submission to God, his head, for a woman to remain in her proper place. In I Corinthians 11:4 Paul says, *"Every man praying or prophesying, having his head covered, dishonoureth his head."* Paul is telling the men that if you pray or prophesy while your hair is uncut then you have not only dishonored your physical head but your spiritual head as well. The spiritual head of the man is Christ. When a man tries to pray to God while his hair is uncut, he is actually telling God that he is not interested in remaining submitted to His authority. Children who are completely rebellious to parents usually wind up in trouble. We must remember that if we want all the promises, blessings, and protection that God has for us we must remain submitted to His authority.

There should be no debate about whether Paul is speaking of cutting or not cutting the hair when he uses the word "covering." The next scripture clarifies the meaning of a covering. I Corinthians 11:5-6 states, *"But every woman that prayeth or prophesyeth with her head uncovered dishonoureth her head: for that is even all one as if she were shaven. For if the woman be not covered, let her also be shorn: but if it be a shame for a woman to be shorn or shaven, let her be covered."* Paul clearly shows us that the word "cover" refers to the woman's hair being uncut. It is not the length of hair that God is concerned with; it is the condition of the hair being cut or uncut. Women of different race and culture may have hair that only grows to a certain length while others may have hair that can grow to enormously long lengths. God did not specify a certain length to be

Then why does it mention long hair for a covering?

Greek word for covering here is Katalalupto which means to cover or veil (clothes) Peribolaion has used describing covering of long hair which means to wrap (clothes)

in submission to authority. He simply says He is looking for cut versus uncut! If I took hair that was extremely long and cut off approximately one inch, we would probably agree that the hair was still long in length. If I cut off another two inches, we would probably still say it was long. The question is, when does is it become short? In God's eyes it became short the instant it was cut. This is very important for us to understand or we can try and justify why we do certain things. Don't justify trimming your hair by saying that it's still long. According to I Corinthians 11:5-6, if you cut your hair, then in the sight of God you should just go ahead and shave it all off.

During the Bible days if someone had their hair shaved off, it was a shame and embarrassment to them. In Isaiah 3:24, Isaiah prophesies the fall of Judah. He tells them that because of their rebellion towards God, He will cause a scab to come upon the crown of the heads of the daughters of Zion (verse 17). Instead of "well set hair," there will be baldness. We must truly understand and obey the scripture concerning our proper place of authority and the condition of our hair. When a woman prays or teaches with her head uncovered, or cut, then she dishonors not only her physical head but her spiritual head, the man, as well. We could dedicate an entire book to the subject of the importance of submission to authority. However, let me say that if you desire peace, contentment, happiness, joy, strength, the promise of health, long life, a great marriage, children who are in submission to your own authority, power with God, power over the enemy, all the promises in the Word of God, and financial peace in your life, then a woman must remain in submission to her husband and through him to God. In Jeremiah 7:28-29, Jeremiah prophesies to Judah concerning the nation's disobedience. He says because they disobeyed the voice of the Lord (or rebelled), they should just cut off their hair and throw it away. His prophesy refers to Judah and Israel as women who are a shame to Him, so the evidence of their rebellion would be the cutting of their hair. It is very important that women show that they are submitted to the authority in their lives by not cutting their hair and men do the same by cutting their hair.

In I Corinthians 11:7-9, Paul gives us an understanding of Genesis 1:27 and why we were created distinctly male and female. *"For a man indeed ought not to cover his head, forasmuch as he is the image and glory of God: but the woman is the glory of the man."* Once again Paul restates that man should have his hair cut because he is created in the image of God and should reflect His glory. Genesis 1:26 states that God created man in his likeness or image. We are the only creation on earth that is made like He is in heaven. God intends for a man to show forth His glory and power by maintaining his male defined status. Then in Genesis 2:21-23, God created woman. Paul restates the order of authority by saying that the woman is the glory of the man. Woman was created from the man's body, so she was created to walk beside a man to help him and reflect his glory. In other words, what I do represents my husband. I Corinthians 11:8-9 states, *"For the man is not of the woman; but the woman of the man. Neither was the man created for the woman; but the woman for the man."* We know this statement is true because of Genesis. God created the man for His glory and then created the woman from the man for the man's glory. This is the order of God and no matter how much you want to kick against it, you will never change His spiritual and physical order.

However, the Lord gave women some power as well. In the Garden of Eden the serpent came to the woman and caused her to sin first. But the Lord, understanding Eve's fall from grace, also gave her a special place in subjecting Satan. First, in Genesis 3:15, God promises Satan that the seed of a woman (prophesying the birth of Jesus) will bruise his head. Satan would bruise the heel of the seed (prophesying the death of Jesus on Calvary) but then the seed would bruise the head of Satan (the resurrection of Jesus Christ). Then in I Corinthians 11:10 Paul states, *"For this cause ought the woman to have power on her head because of the angels."* If a woman remains in submission to God's chain of authority (God-man-woman) by not cutting her hair, then she becomes a curse to Satan. Remember that his fall was all about rebellion to authority, and when we remain submitted to authority, we bring new condemnation upon his kingdom. Each time I worship in church with my hair uncut, I again condemn Satan for his fall from heaven, his temptation of Eve, and his rebellion against God. I am also a sign to the angels that remain in heaven about the joy that is in a submitted life. I am glad to know that each day I can condemn the devil and witness to the angels just through my submission to authority.

In I Corinthians 11:11-12, Paul tells the man and woman that they need each other for the chain of authority to continue correctly. *"Nevertheless neither is the man without the woman, neither the woman without the man, in the Lord. For as the woman is of the man, even so is the man also by the woman; but all things of God."* God has a divine purpose for men and women, but we have to remain in our proper place in the chain of authority for our purpose to be fulfilled. God created us to need each other and to work together to build a family and the kingdom of God. He lets us know that He created all things, but He created them to work together in the proper order. In the spiritual world the man and the woman need each other to make it all work. Also in the physical world, the woman would never have existed except God created her from man; neither would men exist in the world today without a woman to give birth to them. We depend on each other for our very existence, so why would we not subject ourselves to God's order?

In the next few scriptures Paul talks about what nature teaches us. I Corinthians 11:13-15 states, *"Judge in yourselves: is it comely that woman pray unto God uncovered? Does not even nature itself teach you, that, if a man have long hair, it is a shame unto him? But if a woman have long hair, it is a glory to her: for her hair is given her for a covering."* Paul wraps up this entire sermon about hair with a statement on our natural inclinations concerning hair. When we see two people walking with their backs turned towards us, both with long hair, our first thought is "women." Many times I have been shocked to realize that one or both of them were men. We instinctively view long hair as being a female attribute and short hair as a male attribute. It is not that we are trained that way, but God created that nature within us. Likewise women who have really short hair can be mistake for men at times. Our hair is our glory, and it represents our covering in the chain of God's authority. We must make sure that we are obedient to the Word of God. In I Corinthians 11:2, Paul refers to the way we keep our hair as ordinances or laws. He is instructing us on how to be pleasing to God and maintain our relationship with Him.

One of my greatest frustrations as a pastor's wife is the abuse of I Corinthians 11:16. Many people use this scripture to justify cutting their hair. It states: *"But if any man seem to be contentious, we have no such custom, neither the churches of God."* Some people want to interpret this scripture to mean that if anyone has a problem with Paul's instructions concerning our hair, just do what you want to do. I don't see where in any of Paul's other writings, he would give a sermon on how to live correctly and then seem to change his mind. God did not have Paul write I Corinthians 11:1-15 and then in verse 16 tell us that if we don't agree with him, just toss out verses 1-15. My Bible says that God does not change! The interpretation of this scripture is simply this. If anyone wants to argue about this issue just tell them this is how Christians live and do things. The greatest translation that I have ever seen of this scripture is found in The Promise Bible: Contemporary English Version (Thomas Nelson, Publisher). It says, **"This is how things are done in all of God's churches, and that's why none of you should argue about what I have said."** It is not an "out" to do what you want; in fact, it is just the opposite. Paul says this is how we live as Christians so just quit arguing and obey the Word of God!

The Historical Perspective[1]

The cutting of women's hair began with the advent of the movie industry and the Women's Rights Movement in the 1920's. During this era when the men were going to war and the women were taking on the men's jobs, women went into barber shops and asked for a "bob." The term "bob" was used because it changed a woman's hair from looking female to looking male, and they used a

---

[1] Much of the historical facts regarding hair came from Penny Watkins' book *A Hair Short of Glory* (Word Aflame Press, 1996).

man's name for the haircut. Men didn't even know how to cut women's hair, so they would simply cut it straight along the bottom and straight above the eyes. That is the traditional "bob" cut. At the same time that women began cutting their hair, they also began to shorten their skirts, tear out the sleeves (the first sleeveless dresses), and add much ornamentation (bangles and fringe in gold and silver) to the hem, neckline, and sleeves of the dress. Look at dresses during the flapper era. The cutting of the hair came from the Women's Liberation Movement. Isn't it amazing that they would call it "liberation" when that was exactly what they were doing? They were liberating themselves from submission to God's chain of authority. Don't get confused; you can feel a great spirit of liberty when you cut ties with God. But that is just temporary. When you need God's mercy, God's protection, and God's promises, that's when that liberty becomes your curse. It is better to stay submitted to God now and have access to all of His Word. An amazing statistic is that in 1922 there were 5,000 beauty shops, and in the next two years there were 23,000. By the year 1924, 70% of all women in New York had bobbed their hair.

If you still don't believe that hair is a sign of a woman's submission to God, let me take you to the 1960's. Even modern historians agree that this was the age of rebellion. People rebelled against the law, against the war, against government, against their parents and against all morality and decency of that day (the Sexual Revolution). During this time we saw an amazing trend. Women cut their hair extremely short. In fact the most famous woman's haircut of that day was the pixie cut. It was cut so short that there was no hair below the back of the neck. At the same time that women were cutting their hair to look like men, men were growing their hair out as a sign of rebellion. The look of the 60's for men was hair below the shoulder blades, unkempt, with long sideburns and mustaches. These people didn't even understand that they were rebelling against a spiritual precept.

Here are some reasons why we obey I Corinthians 11:1-16:

1. It is a sign of our submission to the chain of God's authority;

2. It demonstrates a wife's submission to her husband and then to God;

3. It demonstrates a husband's submission to God;

4. It is a sign upon the head of a woman to the angels to remain in submission to God's authority;

5. It is a condemnation to Satan and his angels that we remain in good standing with God because of our submission;

6. It continues the distinction that God set up in Genesis 1:27 of male and female;

7. It is shameful for a man to approach God in prayer with uncut hair;

8. It is a glory for a woman to approach God with her hair uncut;

9. Nature teaches us what is right; and

10. As long as we remain in submission to God we have access to all the promises given us in the Word of God.

SEVENTEEN

Modern Media

Satan's Tools

The greatest tool that Satan has ever had is modern media. It has been the single most effective cultural thermostat there is. The difference between a thermometer and a thermostat is that a thermometer simply measures the temperature, but the thermostat actually sets the temperature. Television, movies, magazines, books, and radio have radically changed the culture in which we live today. Every day the devil blasts his message through every media. We cannot enter a store without hearing his music or seeing his message. Our children, our teens, and our adults are desensitized by the bombarding messages of premarital sex, homosexuality, violence, and self-gratification. It is vital that we keep our hearts right with God and limit our intake of media. Job 31:1 explains it best by saying, *"I made a covenant with mine eyes...."*

I would ask you the question "Is sin in technology?" What is worse -- a television or a telephone? Technology is not the problem; the problem is the heart of man. Look at Eve. She committed the first sin, and she didn't even have a television, a telephone, or a *Cosmopolitan* magazine! If your heart is wicked, you will find a way to sin with or without technology. Many churches don't have televisions; however, they have telephones that are used for gossip and tearing down the church. Man has been sinning from the beginning before any technology was available.

We must make a choice to commit ourselves to the Lord completely and subject our flesh to what we know is right. We must guard our hearts, minds, ears, and eyes from sin that is made accessible to us via all types of media: telephone, television, computer, magazines, and books. One is no worse than another, and all can be abused. Remember that change begins inwardly but produces outward fruit.

In Psalm 101:3, David says, *"I will set no wicked thing before mine eyes: I hate the work of them that turn aside; it shall not cleave to me."* The term "wicked" is interpreted in the Hebrew to mean "thing of Belial or Satan." I don't think we have to watch television, be on a computer, pick up a magazine, or open a book to understand that these can be Satan's tools. He uses these things to promote his ideology and doctrine. The apostle Paul was very clear on what we should be focusing our mind. In Philippians 4:8 he instructs us, *"Finally, brethren, whatsoever things are true, whatsoever things are honest, whatsoever things are just, whatsoever things are pure, whatsoever things are lovely, whatsoever things are of good report; if there be any virtue, and if there be any praise, think on these things."* Our job is to keep our mind under control and subjected to the Spirit of God.

In Psalm 119:37 David prays, *"Turn away mine eyes from beholding vanity...."* I need the help of the Lord in my life to be able to overcome the influence of this world. Isaiah explained that by guarding our eyes and ears we could actually dwell in the presence of God, have a strong defense, be sustained with bread, and be sure. Isaiah 33:15-16 states, "He that walketh righteously, and speaketh uprightly; he that despiseth the gain of oppressions, that shaketh his hands from holding of bribes, that stoppeth his ears from hearing of blood, and shutteth his eyes from seeing evil; He shall dwell on high: his place of defence shall be the munitions of rocks: bread shall be given him; his waters shall be sure." This scripture indicates that we make the choice to participate in or to abstain from these evils.

There are many media outlets that we could participate in and perhaps would not be sin; however, in everything we do we are a witness of God. I Thessalonians 5:22 tells us to abstain from the very "appearance of evil." I believe that we must be careful that our witness does not receive irreparable damage from our actions.

The condition of our inward man is reflected in our outward man. In Matthew 15:18-20 and Mark 7:21-23, Jesus explains that things from within come out and defile us. Here's a list of items that He says come from within an unguarded heart and proceed out: "evil thoughts, murders, adulteries, fornications, thefts, false witness, [and] blasphemies." It's like reading the latest movie script from Hollywood. We must be wiser than a serpent and understand that all these things are simply tools for Satan to plant his ideology in the hearts and minds of men. If he can get a person full of these sinful ideas, then that person will eventually produce those ideas outwardly. Proverbs 23:7 confirms that "as a man thinking in his heart, so is he."

The world understands the power of what we see. That is why we have sayings like, "the eyes are the windows of the soul" and "a picture is worth a thousand words." We can see the power of what we see in the coverage of World War I and II and the Gulf and Iraqi Wars. Modern America can see each battle as if they are there via television, magazines, and the Internet instead of waiting months to see a grainy, black and white photo of what is happening on the other side of the world. We are bombarded each day with images, and we must make sure that we are following Paul's advice about absorbing information that is true, honest, pure, lovely, and of a good report!

Radio, Television, and Film

Let's take a look at the history of radio, television, and movies. Each was created with a good intention -- improving communication. They were intended to bring people from all around the world closer together by being able to communicate faster and clearer. Radio was used to tell America that Japan had bombed Pearl Harbor, television sent the first images of a man walking on the moon, and even documentary films have shared the images of Nazi death camps during World War II.

Television was first seen at the 1939 World Fair, but regularly broadcasted programming did not begin until the 1940's. At first, no one thought television would be that big of a deal, but quickly people began to change their minds. In the 1950's the teachers, parents, and social scientists put out a statement warning against the violence that could be seen on TV. I'm amazed that there was such concern about the possible effects of television during the 1950's. I wonder what those same people would say about the programming on television today.

Our society has become so consumed by this media. The following are just a few alarming statistics concerning television:

1. During the elementary years of a child, they will have seen over 20,000 murders and 80,000 other assaults.

2. By the time a student graduates high school they will have spent 11,000 hours in school and 15,000 hours watching TV.

3. Students who are heavy TV watchers (four or more hours per day) are poor readers, bad students, don't play well with friends, have fewer hobbies and activities and are more likely to be overweight.

4. 20 to 25 violent acts will be committed every hour on Saturday morning "children's programs."

5. TV has shortened our attention spans.

6. TV is a thief of time. The average person watches 50,000 to 75,000 hours of TV in his lifetime. That's 5-8 years of his life spent in front of a tube.

Social scientists have identified three effects of television violence on viewers:

1. They become less sensitive to pain and suffering in others;
2. They are more fearful of the world around them; and
3. They are more aggressive and more likely to harm others.

Television is sending an immoral message to our children today. It says that homosexuality is just another lifestyle and can even be funny. It leaves out the horrors of AIDS and the loneliness of the homosexual lifestyle. And yet this is one of the most popular causes promoted by actors and sitcoms. Slowly and surely television is desensitizing our children to the consequences of the homosexual lifestyle.

The media in general advocates pre-marital sex (fornication) and teaches our children that it is okay and safe. It is taught in school and through the media that there are no consequences for fornicating. It makes those who remain pure seem not normal and weird. Every night on television there are numerous people engaging in this behavior. What example do we want our children to follow? We must control their intake of television and movies, as well as other media such as magazines and books.

The media tells us that adultery and multiple relationships are part of a normal life. It doesn't expose the emotional damage adultery produces in a marriage and in the lives of the children involved. Instead it gives awards to soap opera stars who have been married nine times or more on their shows. We must see the danger of allowing our lives to be consumed by this ideology.

The key to all media is the heart. Your pastor cannot write laws of holiness in your heart. He can control what is on his platform at church, but if your heart is determined to do evil, then you will. Be like Job and make a covenant with your eyes. Love God enough to focus on good things and abstain from evil things. I believe that every Christian needs to control what they see and hear through television, the telephone, the computer, movies, books, and magazines. If you are absorbing too much of the world and not the Word, then you need to clean up your act and get your heart right with God.

EIGHTEEN

Makeup

The Biblical Perspective

The Bible tells us in Genesis 1 that we were made in the image of God. We were created to reflect to the world His image and His glory. Everything we do in our outward appearance reflects either His image or an image of the world. We must continually look at each aspect of our outward image and make sure that we are shining forth His true light.

In the Bible, a woman painting her face is noted as a harlot or a prostitute. A woman would paint her face or eyelids specifically to attract attention and entice someone. Never in the Bible does a woman paint her face to entice the presence of the Lord. In fact, in I Peter 3:3 the Bible says, *"Whose adorning let it not be that outward adorning of plaiting the hair, and of wearing of gold, or of putting on of apparel; But let it be the hidden man of the heart, in that which is not corruptible, even the ornament of a meek and quiet spirit, which is in the sight of God of great price."* The purpose of make-up is to alter a person's appearance to entice someone. It is a tool to draw attention to ourselves simply for the sake of vanity. We must make sure that we are being careful to desire only the attention of God on our lives and be pleasing to Him.

In II Kings 9:30, Jezebel painted her face to try to entice Jehu and keep him from killing her. Somewhere in Jezebel's life this ploy had worked before, and here she was trying it again. In Proverbs 6:24-26, the Bible speaks of the adulteress and not allowing her to "take you with her eyes." It lets us know that this woman was trying to destroy something precious by enticing someone with her looks. Jeremiah 4:30 says, "And when thou art spoiled, what wilt thou do? Though thou clothest thyself with crimson, though thou deckest thee with ornaments of gold, though thou rentest thy face with painting, in vain shalt thou make thyself fair; thy lovers will despise thee, they will seek thy life." The person of whom Jeremiah speaks painted her face and tried to make herself beautiful for her lovers. Read Ezekial 23:40-49. The painting of the eyes is used to describe Israel and Judah as two adulterous sisters. In the Bible the Lord always uses make-up in conjunction with the sin of lust. Remember the purpose of holiness is to be accepted into His presence and to be holy as He is holy.

In the book of Esther, a young Jewish girl is among the candidates chosen to be the new queen. She endures separation from family, a year long purification process, and then it is time for her to go in unto the king. Esther 2:13 tells us that as each maiden's turn comes to go in to see the king, she is given the opportunity to choose whatever adornment she wanted or felt she needed. In Esther 2:15 the Bible tells us that Esther "required nothing" before approaching the king. Matthew Henry's commentary[2] states it this way:

> *She was not solicitous, as the rest of the maidens were, to set herself off with artificial beauty; she required nothing but just what was appointed for her (v. 15) and yet she was most acceptable. The more natural beauty is the more agreeable.*

This story is a great analogy of holiness. Esther's whole objective was to be pleasing and accepted by the king. Our responsibility is to be pleasing and accepted by our King. He created us as we are, and we need to be careful not to pick up the ideas of the world on beauty. David acknowledged the perfection of God's creation in Psalm 13:13-16:

> For you created my inmost being; you knit me together in my mother's womb. I praise you because I am fearfully and wonderfully made; your works are wonderful, I know that

---

[2] *Matthew Henry's Commentary on the Whole Bible: New Modern Edition, Electronic Database. Copyright © 1991 by Hendrickson Publishers, Inc.*

full well. My frame was not hidden from you when I was made in the secret place. When I was woven together in the depths of the earth, your eyes saw my unformed body. All the days ordained for me were written in your book before one of them came to be. (NIV)

God made us and knows how well we are made! We are each beautiful and wonderfully made before Him. We must seek to draw His attention through our meek and gentle spirit, our praise and worship, and our love of being holy as He is holy. We should avoid using the outward trappings of the world to become its idea of beauty.

The Historical Perspective

In the 1920's when the movie industry began, all pictures were in black and white. So to be able to make the actresses' and actors' faces stand out, they had to apply enormous amounts of make-up. One actress in particular was famous for introducing the practice of wearing make-up off the set and into public. Her name was Theda Bara and her nickname was "Vampire." She was given this name not as it relates to the story of Dracula, but because she was said to seduce and destroy men on screen. Movie theaters were packed each night to watch her "vamp" another young man. She influenced women of that day to throw moral caution to the wind, paint their faces with extreme make-up and go out on the town for a night of "vamping."

Any Christian should be able to understand that this is not an influence that we should follow. We should reflect the morals of Christ and not the world.

The original use of make-up dates back to Egyptian times. A heavy, dark make-up, called "kohl" was used to outline the tops and bottoms of the eyelids. Any woman made up in this manner signaled to men that she was a prostitute and available.

In the Bible, Egypt was a type of the world and sin and slavery. After experiencing God's freedom, why would anyone want to remain in bondage to the world and sin? God separates us to be His witness and His people just as He did the children of Israel.

Realize that the spirit of make-up is not from God. It indicates a spirit of lust and adultery according to the Word of God. The use of make-up comes from a long history of prostitution and, in the more recent past, the movie industry. God made us in His image and desires for our appearance to reflect His glory at all times. It is important that we understand the motivating factors behind an issue and determine whether or not it is good for us to be involved in that issue. Make-up has become a tool Satan uses to convince women, in particular, that they are not beautiful as God created them. We must be careful not to fall into his trap of worldly ideology. Let our appearance reflect the glory of God completely.

NINETEEN

Jewelry

The Biblical Perspective

Our motivation for doing the things we do to our appearance is a great issue with God. I Samuel 16:7 shows us that He knows our hearts and what motivates us. The outward beauty of Jesse's sons impressed Samuel but not God; God was concerned more with the condition of the heart of a man and how it reflected Him outwardly.

Throughout the Bible we see many references to jewelry; however, anytime God wanted His people to draw closer to Him or be more consecrated to Him, He asked them to remove their jewelry. In Genesis 35:1-7, God desires Jacob to draw closer to Him, so Jacob makes some changes in his camp.

"And God said unto Jacob, Arise, go up to Bethel, and dwell there: and make there an altar unto God, that appeared unto thee when thou fleddest from the face of Esau thy brother.

Then Jacob said unto his household, and to all that were with him, Put away the strange gods that are among you, and be clean, and change your garments:

And let us arise, and go up to Bethel; and I will make there an altar unto God, who answered me in the day of my distress, and was with me in the way which I went.

And they gave unto Jacob all the strange gods which were in their hand, and all their earrings which were in their ears; and Jacob hid them under the oak which was by Shechem.

And they journeyed: and the terror of God was upon the cities that were round about them, and they did not pursue after the sons of Jacob.

So Jacob came to Luz, which is in the land of Canaan, that is, Bethel, he and all the people that were with him.

And he built there an altar, and called the place El-beth-el: because there God appeared unto him, when he fled from the face of his brother."

God wanted Jacob to build Him an altar or a place where He could commune with (or be closer to) Jacob. The people took off those things which represented the world and went into the presence of the Lord clean. So our first conclusion concerning jewelry is that putting it off helps us to draw closer to the presence of God. In Romans 12:1, Paul tells us to "present our bodies, a living sacrifice, holy, acceptable unto God." Holiness is taking our body and making it acceptable to the presence of the Lord. He desires us to put off some things so that we can be allowed into His presence.

Let us recall for a moment the illustration of Mount Sinai used in the previous chapters of this book. The Lord tells Moses that the people are not allowed to even touch the mountain where His presence is being displayed in thunder and lightening. Exodus 19:18-25 is the story of God telling Moses not to allow the people into His presence. The Lord lets Moses know in verse 22 that the people needed to be "sanctified" or cleansed before they could come into His presence.

Exodus 11 relates the story of the children of Israel leaving Egypt. The Lord instructs them in Exodus 11:2 to collect gold, silver, and jewelry from all their Egyptian neighbors.

First of all, notice that jewelry began in Egypt. The Israelites borrowed the jewelry from the Egyptians -- not the other way around. You never see in the scripture where the Lord tells them to wear the jewelry. In fact, this jewelry causes them to get in trouble in Exodus 32:1-4. The very jewelry that they brought out of the land of Egypt, which was symbolic of them winning a war and spoiling their enemy, they melted into an idol to worship. The main reason that the Lord wanted them to take the jewelry was to make the items needed for worship in the wilderness tabernacle. In Exodus 35:22, they brought all their jewelry to be used to build the tabernacle.

In Judges 8:24, the wearing of earrings identified people as Ishmaelites. Ishmael was the son of Abraham with Hagar, Sarah's Egyptian handmaiden. Ishmael was not the promised son, Isaac, but was actually the disobedience of Abraham and Sarah. Instead of waiting on God to fulfill His promise to them, they took the promise into their own hands. Today we still reap the pain of this decision because the dissention between the Israelites (children of Isaac) and the Arab nations (children of Ishmael) continues to affect our lives.

When Gideon asked the children of Israel in Judges 8:24-27 to give him the earrings of their prey, it wasn't for a good reason. In fact we see that his obtaining this jewelry caused him to sin, and in turn, he caused Israel to sin. Once again the people wearing the jewelry were not the children of God, but they were actually known as the children of the world by the jewelry they wore. Our responsibility in holiness is to reflect the image of God.

We are identified by what we wear. Others will know to whom we belong and whom we represent by what we wear. Jeremiah 4:30 not only speaks of make-up but also of the harlot that adorned herself with gold to attract the attention of many lovers. She was showing these men that she wasn't an ordinary woman, but was available for other uses. We must be careful because we can take the ornaments of the world and try to represent Christ. I Peter 3:3

tells us to not let our adorning be with the outward wearing of gold, but to let our appearance show that we represent Jesus Christ. Ezekiel 23:40 also tells the story of another harlot who adorned herself with ornaments meant to attract attention to herself.

In Hosea 2:13, the Lord gives a prophecy concerning Israel. He explains that in the days of Baalim, when Israel was turning away from Him, they did a few things. The woman to which He refers is Israel. She decked herself out with jewelry and went after other gods. She was playing a harlot and adulteress in the sight of God.

The Historical Perspective

In studying the history of jewelry, we don't really see many references to people wearing anything until the time of the Egyptians. Before that time it was mostly shells or rocks that people would wear around their necks or arms. Most jewelry that originally was worn was used to show that they worshipped a certain god. In Egypt the sun god, Ra, was worshipped by wearing a sunburst carved into gold on your arm, neck, or head. The Pharaoh and those of his household wore a lot of jewelry in the form of signet rings, wide collared necklaces that covered them down to their chests, golden crowns and head pieces, bracelets of gold around their upper arm and their lower wrist, and many other smaller types of jewelry. They wore these things to represent their personal wealth, their position above all the other people and as talismans to ward off evil.

Throughout the rest of history, through the ages of the Greeks, the Byzantine Empire, the development of Europe, the discovery of America and down to present times, jewelry has continued to be used to show wealth, power, and position. Henry VIII of England had the most opulent collection of jewelry. His daughter, Elizabeth I, loved wearing large amounts of jewelry all over her body. During this time there was a great separation between the rich aristocrats and the poor. It was also during this time that King Louis XIV of France and his queen, Marie Antoinette, caused the French Revolution due to their personal opulence while the rest of the country was so poor they could not eat.

Jewelry was also used as a tool to keep slaves bound together. They would create a necklace of steel, gold, or iron and place a ring in the front. They would create similar items for the wrist and feet. Then they would string the slaves together in a long line and make them walk. It was a way to make sure that no one escaped; however, if by chance someone got away everyone would know they were a slave by the necklace, bracelet, or anklet.

In the Bible Egypt is used as a type of sin or the world. When God brought the children of Israel out of Egypt, the first place He took them was to Mount Sinai to show them how they could be accepted into His presence. He was very specific that they were going to have to put off the patterns, styles, and conduct that they had learned while living in Egypt 400 years. When God saves us from this world there should be transformation in our lives according to Romans 12:2. We should not act, walk, talk, or look like what God saved us from. In Egypt the Israelites were bound together as slaves. They had no personal or religious freedom. They lived according to the dictates of Pharaoh and their Egyptian masters. God even told Moses and Aaron to tell Pharaoh to let His people go so they could "worship" Him in the wilderness. Obviously they had been hindered from truly "worshipping" God the way they wanted to in Egypt.

History shows us that the true start of jewelry came with the Egyptian kingdom and was used as a way to worship all their gods. The one true and living God shows us through His Word that each time He wanted someone to draw closer to Him, He requested they take off their jewelry and other things that represented the world.

Finally, what is our motivation or purpose for wearing jewelry? That outward adornment is not for the eyes of God, but rather to attract the eyes of man. My purpose in this world is to be a witness of Him and show who I truly belong to. I want the world to look at me and see a difference. I want them to realize that I am transformed by the power of Jesus Christ. If you want to draw closer to the presence of God, then you will put off things that could stand in your way. It won't be a sacrifice to put those things down, but rather a privilege to come into His holy presence and commune with Him.

TWENTY

Tattoos & Piercings

The Biblical Perspective

Many years ago the inclusion of this topic in a book on holiness may not have been necessary, due to the fact that this was not prevalent in our society. However, when you look around and see the increase of people getting both tattoos and piercings, we have to define the Biblical standard and our cultural trend to be able to speak definitively on this topic.

Leviticus 19:28 says, *"Ye shall not make any cuttings in your flesh for the dead, nor print any marks upon you: I am the Lord."* Remember when God originally called Abraham, He asked that he come out from the people around him and be separate (different). The pagan people of that day used tattoos to try and appease the god's and get help for loved ones who had died. God had asked His people to not be like others and this was to keep them separated unto Him and for His glory. In fact, by keeping our bodies clean and unmarked, we show that we are truly His and belong to Him.

In 1 Corinthians 3:17 we also see the scripture underline this point regarding ownership of our bodies. *"If any many defile the temple of God, him shall God destroy; for the temple of God is holy, which temple ye are."* We would be horrified if we saw someone come into our church and begin to spray graffiti on the walls, but this is how God feels when we mark up His temple – our bodies. I Corinthians 6:19-20 continues to explain this by saying, *"What? Know ye not that your body is the temple of the Holy Ghost which is in you, which ye have of God, and ye are not your own? For ye are bought with a price: therefore glorify God in your body, and in your spirit, which are God's."* When you receive His Spirit you no longer belong to yourself but you have become His house, His temple, His dwelling place. Therefore remember that marking your body is defacing His property. He wants us to represent Him and be separate from the rest of the world.

The Historical Perspective

When you read about the history of tattooing you will realize that it always had some sort of spiritual reasoning behind it. Some of the first tattoos were seen on mummified bodies from Egypt. The tattoos represented markings for loved ones that were given to help the god's accept them into the afterlife. They were used as protection against evil spirits. They believed that if they were tattooed with a symbol of a diety (such as Ra – the sun god), then his enemies would not attack the person. People would be tattooed with the picture of an animal of that day because they believed that that animal would not attack them. Later on during the Greek and Roman eras, people were tattooed to denote them as slaves or criminals. Their crimes and names of their victims would be tattooed in a prominent location so that everyone that met them would know their crime and they could never hide what they had done. Slaves were tattooed so that they could never escape slavery but would always be known by their markings. Even during the time of the settlement of our West, the American Indians would use tattoos to show how many they had killed. Tattoos have been used as good luck charms, to prevent sickness by keeping evil spirits away and to denote their religious beliefs.

The history of piercings dates back also to the cultures of the Old Testament. They would pierce people to show ownership or property. They would require their wives to wear symbols of ownership and the bigger the item placed in either the nose or ear, denoted the wealth of the owner. The modern age of piercing began with the Punk music movement, which began at the end of the 1960's and the beginning of the 1970's. It was their symbol and they told people that it was to show their rebellion against conservative values. Even today, if we see someone with excessive piercings, our first thought is that they are rebellious. It is associated with this overall theme.

Our Perspective

When we look at the Bible and see that we do not belong to ourselves, but we are His temple (dwelling place), we make a choice to be unmarked to represent Him. Then we look at the fact that tattooing and piercing throughout history has always been a sign of pagan religious rituals, slavery and rebellion, then it is clear what our decision must be regarding this behavior.

The Bible also teaches us to take into account the end of things instead of just the beginning. We need to carefully consider how we will feel about what we are doing later on in life. Statistics say that 20-50% of people later in life regret getting a tattoo.

However, I don't think a discussion of this topic would be complete without addressing how we should treat those who are born again out of this world and already have tattoos. Due to the rise of the popularity of tattoos in our culture, we have to realize that we will have many people who will come to God and already have marked their bodies. We can often feel (our traditional values) uncomfortable to use these people in our churches. However, I always keep two things in mind when controlling my thoughts and actions about this. First of all, if God filled them with the Holy Ghost while marked, then I should be careful to not place my opinion higher than His. We can ask them to wear longer sleeves and try to cover as much as they can, but if they are committed, faithful and following Jesus, then we must overcome our own prejudices and issues and allow God to use them.

In Acts 15, a similar issue arose in the new church. Paul & Barnabas had come to share with the apostles in Jerusalem all the good things that had been happening among the Gentiles. While there, the Jewish church members begin to request that the Gentiles be circumcised so that they would be in agreement with Mosaic Law. However, Peter answered them in verses 7-11 by telling them that

God had filled them with the same Holy Ghost without circumcision and therefore we should not put more on them that God would require of them.

Secondly, the Bible tells us that judgment begins at the house of God (1 Peter 4:17). This simply means that when someone comes in and is filled with the Holy Ghost, baptized in His name and walking in the Spirit, we have to cease judging them based on past actions or issues. We have to allow their new life to begin. We have to find a way to overcome *our issues* and allow them to begin anew.

It is easy to ask someone to get rid of their piercings, but tattoos are permanent and hard to get rid of. We do not need to make that a requirement of usefulness or service in the Kingdom of God. We can ask that they cover as much as they can, but we have to train ourselves and teach our people to be Biblical not only in our standard but in our judgment of others as well. If God has forgiven us our issues, which may not be visible but would be just as sinful, then we must forgive others their issues no matter where they manifest themselves.

TWENTY-ONE

Standards Are Our Protection

There are many standards that are set forth in the Word of God. They are given to us for our protection. They are not given to be a prison in our lives. God wants us to have access to everything He has written in the Bible, but we must maintain holiness so that we can be accepted into His presence.

The principle of submission to authority is one that is a theme throughout the Word of God. But we not only have to submit to the authority of the Word, but to our pastor and leadership as well. God has given us shepherds who are given the responsibility of teaching us the Word and helping us continue to walk with God. Many times issues arise that may not be sinful, but a pastor may set standards or boundaries for his flock with their best interest in mind. If our pastor gives us guidelines that we choose not to obey, then the problem is not the issue or standard, but our lack of submission to the authority God has placed in our lives. When a pastor draws a line regarding an issue, at that point every person in that church has to make a choice. They can submit to the admonishment of their pastor or continue to disobey his direction. If they choose to disobey the pastor, the Lord isn't concerned about the issue anymore; He is concerned about that person's rebellious attitude. Each church is different, and different pastors ask different things of us. The most important thing we must do is keep a submitted heart and attitude and allow God to deal with us in our lives.

I was once asked to speak to a group about dealing with holiness problems. My response was that I don't really have holiness problems in my church. Don't get me wrong, there are people who are not submitted to our church's holiness standards, but I don't have to deal with petty arguments and disagreements about holiness. I believe that the cure for holiness problems is proper holiness teaching. If we can get people to understand that the proper order for holiness is a right attitude, understanding God's principles, inward holiness, and then outward holiness, then we can solve a lot of the problems we face in our churches. Many problems are personal disagreements because we don't have the right attitude concerning holiness. I don't have to mediate between women or men in my church. I teach them that we are all in the process of holiness. I may be at mile marker 2,000 while someone else is just starting at mile marker 10. The only thing I am concerned about is the direction the person is moving. As long as the person is moving towards God, then we are okay. The instant that he or she starts moving away from God, we have a problem. I have always taught in our church that my job is to be behind my new converts, encouraging them in the process of holiness. My job is not be in their faces telling them what they do and don't need to do. I may become a stumbling block to them as they are trying to go towards God. However, if I am in my proper place (behind them, encouraging them) in holiness then if they happen to turn around and try to return to world, I can become a stumbling block to their backsliding. It is important that we submit to the Word of God, the authority and command of our pastor, and that we maintain the true order of holiness.

I am doing all that I can to fulfill I Peter 1:16, "Because it is written: Be ye holy, for I am holy." Read this holiness study and then teach this holiness study. Let's strive to be like Jesus.

Recommended Reading

Watkins, Penny. *A Hair Short of Glory.* Hazelwood, MO: Word Aflame Press, 1996.

Pamer, Nan. *I Will Not Bow.* Hazelwood, MO: Word Aflame Press, 1997.

Pamer, Nan. *Modesty.* Hazelwood, MO: Word Aflame Press, 1990.

Bernard, David. *In Search of Holiness.* Hazelwood, MO; Word Aflame Press, ?

Made in USA - Kendallville, IN
12444_9781517636319
05.03.2023 1329